Oswald Crawfurd

English Comic Dramatists

Oswald Crawfurd

English Comic Dramatists

ISBN/EAN: 9783337303181

Printed in Europe, USA, Canada, Australia, Japan

Cover: Foto ©Thomas Meinert / pixelio.de

More available books at **www.hansebooks.com**

COMIC DRAMATISTS

EDITED BY

OSWALD CRAWFURD

LONDON
KEGAN PAUL, TRENCH & CO.
MDCCCLXXXIII

CONTENTS

	Page
SHAKSPERE. 1564—1616	1
King Henry IV—Part First	3
BEN JONSON. 1573—1637	11
The Alchemist	13
The Fox	28
Every Man in his Humour	42
BEAUMONT AND FLETCHER. 1586—1616 : 1579—1625	57
A King and no King	59
WYCHERLEY. 1640—1715	65
The Plain Dealer	67
VANBRUGH. 1666—1726	83
A Journey to London	85

CONTENTS

Page

VANBRUGH. 1666—1726 *(continued)*.

    THE RELAPSE; OR VIRTUE IN DANGER 90

    THE CONFEDERACY 96

COLLEY CIBBER. 1671—1757. 109

    SHE WOU'D AND SHE WOU'D NOT 111

CONGREVE. 1670—1729 129

    THE WAY OF THE WORLD 131

    THE DOUBLE DEALER 145

ADDISON. 1672—1719 161

    THE DRUMMER; OR THE HAUNTED HOUSE. 163

FARQUHAR. 1678—1707 171

    THE BEAUX' STRATAGEM 173

    THE INCONSTANT; OR THE WAY TO WIN HIM . . 178

    THE RECRUITING OFFICER 189

JOHN GAY. 1688—1732 203

    THE BEGGAR'S OPERA 205

GOLDSMITH. 1728—1774 213

    THE GOOD-NATURED MAN 215

    SHE STOOPS TO CONQUER 235

CONTENTS

	Page
CUMBERLAND. 1732—1811	255
THE WEST INDIAN	257
SHERIDAN. 1752—1816	261
THE SCHOOL FOR SCANDAL	263

INTRODUCTION

THE idea which underlies true and pure comedy is, as the present writer understands it, that it should furnish cause for mocking but not ungenial laughter by a representation, in the guise of a fable—interesting dramatically—of the various actions, motives, humours, follies, inconsistencies, absurdities, pretensions, and hypocrisies of human life.

In doing this, which, as man's literary capacity and his faculty of imagination go, seems to be a most difficult and rarely well-done thing, if the mirror be truly held up to nature, the result—after allowing for some slight conventional distortion of the image in accordance with accepted stage traditions—is Comedy, whether it be after the grand fashion set by Shakspere, or in the mode of Molière, or in that of Congreve and Sheridan. If the glamour of romance be cast over a drama, and if the characters, using a poetic diction, address each other otherwise than as men and women do in daily life, it is still indeed comedy in common parlance, because our poverty of language has no exacter word for it: it is a high and beautiful product of human intelligence, but it is not true, pure comedy.

If, on the other hand, the image cast upon the stage be wholly distorted and falsified, and the action and personages of the drama be made laughter-provoking by exaggeration or caricature, the result is no longer comedy but Farce, whether it be the farce of Aristophanes, of Foote, or of Labiche. Again, if the mockery be ungenial, the laughter savage, or mainly cynical and contemptuous, no dramatic quality it may possess will fit it for stage purposes—will humanize it, as it were; it is neither Comedy nor Farce, but Satire, and the work may please a reader, but will not satisfy an audience.

It is well thus to make a somewhat dogmatic definition of Comedy, that the critical reader may know what he is to expect in the following selections from our English Comic Dramatists. He will see at once how far afield his selector has been able to go, and where he has had to draw the line. Having regard only to the providing of good and interesting reading, he might have quoted largely from our Romantic Drama, in which our literature is exceptionally rich, or from our

Farce Drama, to which we have something of an Italian leaning, but to do this would have required folios, not a single small volume.

There is one condition precedent of good comedy the necessity of which cannot be made too clear : it is the pre-existence of a good and a receptive audience. An audience of quick perceptions, among whom a certain education of manners prevails,—an audience ready in the give and take of free social life,—one where women hold a high standing,—an audience critical yet laughter-loving and tolerant,—is the only ground on which the seed of good comedy can germinate and thrive. Such were the audiences that listened to the humours of Ben Jonson and the more natural comedy of Shakspere ; such was the circle, coarse and gross in some respects to our modern apprehension, but wellbred and highly exercised in social converse, which favoured the growth of that 'Restoration Comedy' which for mere wit and brilliancy is the triumph of our Comic Drama. .

After that our star of Comedy was not again in the ascendant till Sheridan's and Goldsmith's time. This later period, too, coincided with a revival of social as well as literary activity, and the fine gentleman manner personified in Lord Chesterfield was still the manner followed by the people who filled the playhouses.

These then are our good comedy periods: Shakspere's period first, then Congreve's, at the head of the Restoration Dramatists, then Sheridan's; after him chaos and anarchy again prevailed in the domain of the Comic Drama.

If we look to the causes of the melancholy *interregna* between these flourishing periods, it will be found to be as often or oftener traceable to the absence of the right conditions afore-mentioned as to the blighting effect of religious bigotry. Twice over, indeed, in our history, as all students of it know, it was this and nothing else which was the cause of deterioration or non-production, for the Puritans actually closed the playhouses in Cromwell's time, and fifty years later the voice of the nonjuring divine, Jeremy Collier, raised in eloquent and not unrighteous protest against the license of the playwrights of the day, went some way to expel wit from the English stage for more than half a century.

Nevertheless, I hold other causes to be even more blighting to comedy than intolerance, and it is a sad admission for Liberals to have to make that mere social liberty is not a thing altogether favourable to good comedy-writing. Unfortunately, the *vox populi* is not the supreme voice in matters dramatical, and it has been but too often raised both to damn a good play (with faint praise or otherwise) and to praise a bad one. This way of accounting for much work that is second-rate in our national comedy will, I think, be seen to hold good if we glance in the most cursory manner at our comedy literature from Shakspere's time.

That austere, passionate, and ardent spirit which made the Elizabethan drama great did not last far into James's or Charles's reigns. It presently died away, and a social relaxation took place, politically desirable, no doubt, for it helped to lead to a more popular civil polity, but for literature unfortunate. Audiences got very easy so long as stage effect and *situation* were attended to. They grew careless of the rest. Beaumont and Fletcher took the place of Shakspere in public estimation, and such clever stage plays as the 'Scornful Lady' and the 'Little French Lawyer,' poor as they are in literature, kept the stage against the greatest of all masters of the drama.

Not till the popular party was in abeyance, and court influence strong again under Charles II., did the Comic Drama revive in new and vigorous form, and

Etheredge, Wycherley, Crowne, and their greater successors, write and flourish. Then came the reaction and Jeremy Collier's wrath, and players and authors alike were shamed or terrified into silence or decorous mediocrity. Not even the wit, learning, and good manners of Queen Anne's reign could avail, and though the Comic Muse ventured to show her face again, it was now much too demure and prudish a face, as a generation before it had been far too brazen a one. It was a modest and moral muse enough that now spoke, but the true mocking spirit of comedy was wanting, the old brilliancy was gone. The best wits of the time could make little of comedy. Steele's and Addison's attempts in that line were not very successful. The moralizing and didactic spirit of the 'Spectator' and the 'Tatler,' with all its neatness, its playfulness, and its delicacy, is not the true comic strain. Addison was once called 'a parson in a tie-wig,' and the sermonizing tendency which the phrase implies is fatal to comedy. His solitary performance in this province, 'The Drummer,' is not a strong performance, while his friend and colleague Steele's earliest and truest comedy, the 'Funeral,' contains little that is good beyond one admirable scene, often quoted, but too short for selection in this work. His most successful piece, the 'Conscious Lovers,' is by common consent of modern critics an insufferably dull comedy.

If comedy could not be revived by the more or less favourable literary conditions of our Augustan age of literature, it was not to be expected that it should flourish when both social life and literature had somewhat degenerated in the reigns of the first Hanoverian sovereigns, and court influence on manners and on the worlds of society and of letters was at its very lowest. The form that comedy took at this stage of its career was after a bad fashion that came from France; and of the so-called Comédie Larmoyante represented with us by Whitchead's 'School for Lovers' and Kelly's 'False Delicacy', one may safely say that the low-water mark of comedy-writing in England was reached. A reaction to a better style began with Garrick himself. By him, and under his auspices as manager of Drury Lane, some of the good Restoration comedies were re-cast and adapted to suit the taste and morals of a politer and more decent age. His and the elder Colman's joint work, 'The Clandestine Marriage,' and Colman's 'Jealous Wife,' are good acting plays which long held the stage. They are, however, hardly more than *rifacimentos* of the Restoration comedies, but they lack the old wit and they lack the old brilliancy of style. I have not found a quotable scene from either. Cumberland was a more original, if a tamer and a more sententious writer. From his 'West Indian' a characteristic scene will be found in the following pages.

The works of these dramatists and of such lesser lights as E. Moore and Murphy were wholly eclipsed by the brilliant dramatic genius of Sheridan, and by the delightful humour of Goldsmith—dramatists wholly dissimilar in manner and in treatment, but both alike in this, that they mainly worked on the lines of Congreve and Farquhar. These two writers are the last of the comedy authors I have quoted from. After their time came a change over English manners. A republican plainness of address, caught from across the Channel, soon to degenerate into awkwardness, not to say sheepishness, banished the old courtly carriage and demeanour from England. Wigs and gold-laced coats, canes and swords, went with our good manners. Every one wore the same coat and affected the same address. In good comedy, gradation and contrasted apposition of manner and of outward bearing and appearance are as much a necessity as in a good picture gradation and apposition of light and shade; but now there was a dull uniformity in life, and nothing left for comedy to make play with. Though there came a reaction presently afterwards, and though some sort of an extravagance in costume and some sort of an extravagant attempt at exclusive manner and address prevailed under the Regency, it was too dull and coarse and gross, too wanting in light and shade and in refinement, to be reproducible in good comedy. It was a society which for stage purposes could only be exaggerated into broad farce; consequently, this was the age of Farce. Comedy was dead.

In making the selections from the Comic Dramatists which are to follow, it has been my endeavour not merely to put together at haphazard a number of comedy scenes that shall amuse and entertain the reader of them, but to give him in a succinct form something which shall thoroughly represent our English comedy literature.

So far as the flavour of a play can be discerned in an extract from it, it is clear that the extract must be one where point and brilliancy of dialogue are preeminent: so far the reader will be fortunate, but he must not go away with the notion that point and brilliancy are all he is to look for in these extracts: there is a good deal more, and that he may appreciate the full difficulty of the selector's task, and not bear too heavily upon his shortcomings, it is well to consider what it is that essentially goes to the making of a good comedy, and how far its essence can be set forth in an extract.

Though I have tried to show what conditions of cultivation, taste, and manners make comedy a possibility, human nature is after all not so compliant as always to supply the comedy-writer, even when everything is quite ready for him; nor is this at all surprising if we consider how much and what difficult work he must include within the narrow limits of a comedy. For, first, he must possess one of the rarest of human faculties, that of moving intelligent laughter— a faculty which some of our most famous playwrights, in past times, have signally lacked, though they have written so-called comedies.

A wit in social life is admittedly a rarity,—a man, that is, who can keep a company in a roar under the immediate stimulus of present social sympathy and immediate social triumph; but the comedy-writer must do as much as this quietly and sadly at his desk with no stimulus at all, and he must do much more, for while he plays the wit's part at one moment, in the next he must play the dullard's and the butt's who is to suffer defeat at his own hands, or, harder still, he must double his own part and be the speaker whose greater wit caps his own first effort; and when all is done that wit and epigram can do, no way at all hardly is made with the comedy unless all these intellectual fireworks are homogeneous to the play, promote its plot, or set forth its purpose. Yet in this first essential of natural, telling, pungent dialogue, how seldom is the mark hit even by our better stage authors! However, it will be apparent to the reader who has agreed with me so far, that wit alone, the mere passing scintillations of pointed shrewdness, mere 'intellectual gladiatorship,' delightful quality as it is, is not, dramatically speaking, the form of wit which is serviceable on the stage, nor is it that alone which shall be found in the following illustrations of our English Comic Drama. What actors want, and audiences too, if they but knew their own minds, is a wit that helps the play on, that releases the springs of the plot, or that reveals a character as in a flash of light; a wit that serves the true purposes of comedy by mocking and marking the odd humours of the characters of the play, a wit shrewd and biting like Benedick's or Falstaff's, broad as humanity itself, and always bearing on the movement of the piece—or an illustrative, picturesque, and passionate wit, as in Congreve's play, where Lady Wishfort, losing her temper and her manners, breaks out into that famous diatribe upon her treacherous maid.

These instances, to be sure, show wit only in the broader and older sense of that word. In our days the thing has been narrowed till it is no longer identical with the French *esprit*, and can best be defined, as a most excellent critic has defined it, "as the sudden discovery of a resemblance between things seemingly unlike." Yet, even taking this definition as right, then the scene in Vanbrugh's 'Confederacy,' where Brass, who has throughout been the subservient friend and confederate of Dick Amlet, a bolder rogue than himself, and has passed for his servant, suddenly at a critical moment asserts his equality and terrifies his confederate into exorbitant terms : if Hazlitt's definition be correct, then this admirable passage—which will be found in the following pages—is nothing but the purest wit in action. Indeed, most of the great situations in comedy—the screen scene in the 'School for Scandal,' Portia's turning of the tables upon Shylock, Prince Henry's discovery of himself to Falstaff— are nothing but this same practical form of wit—wit in action—its most useful form for the stage.

The skilful employment in the face of an audience —who may be described as an assemblage of human beings one half of whom are always wanting to yawn and the other half to hiss—of this form of practical wit would seem to be about the rarest feat in literature. No one who has travelled and re-travelled through some hundreds of plays in a brief space of time—as the present writer has—can fail to be impressed with this fact; and the same person will be inclined to scepticism when he hears talk of the 'palmy days of the Drama' and lamentations over modern degeneracy. Such a traveller in the realms of Dramatic Literature knows of no palmy days, no generation—not even excepting the Cavalier period and its outcome—in which good actable plays were so numerous as the present. We forget that the dozen or so of notable comic dramatists we have in our annals have taken nearly three hundred years to live in. There is still another point to set to modern credit. If some of the older writers infinitely surpass us in wit, in style, and in ease of dialogue, we have left them behind us in all else that goes to the making of a good play. A good actable comedy with literary excellence in it is certainly about the very rarest of literary products, and it appears to the present writer that it is so simply because it is a work of art with the artifice of it carried in three separate directions, and because it is rare to find in a single author the faculty of excursion in three separate directions.

These three requirements would seem to be—first, that the plot should be good,—in other words, that a fresh and interesting story should be expressed to the audience in an intelligible, natural, and entertaining manner; secondly, that this same plain and intelligible plot should possess the almost contrary attribute of ramifying, enlarging, and developing itself as it goes forward and in accordance with certain accepted laws of stage craft, into a succession of unexpected and essentially dramatic situations, each one of them culminating in interest till the final disentanglement of the plot and play.

It is clear that, of these two requirements going to make the ideally perfect comedy, neither can be fairly represented in an extract; but the third requirement can, and the third is that afore-mentioned quality of wit in action, and expressed in epigrammatic dialogue.

It is this chiefly which I have endeavoured to exhibit in these selections from the English Comic Dramatists.

The reader who has followed this introduction so far, and who appreciates its arguments, will agree in the omission of extracts from comedies written before Shakspere's time and after that of Sheridan.

Each scene from a play is preceded by a sketch of the plot sufficient to make the scene intelligible. A short critical note upon each of the dramatists quoted will also be found in the body of the work.

OSWALD CRAWFURD.

SHAKSPERE

BORN 1564.   DIED 1616.

SHAKSPERE'S comedy is, in its way, supreme as his tragedy is supreme, and if but a single specimen of it is given, there is more than one reason for omission. The chief one is that his best scenes are too well known; another is that, as Mr. Swinburne happily says, in Shakspere's plays 'comedy is as inextricably blended with tragedy as it is in real life.' They cannot be separated. A further reason is, that so much of his comedy is so exquisitely imbued with a poetic spirit, that a mere reader—not one of an audience—may well forget the playwright in the poet; and this circumstance—if the rigid definition of comedy with which my introduction sets out is to hold good—would remove Shakspere into a different and a higher sphere than that occupied by the mere comic dramatist.

SHAKSPERE

KING HENRY IV.—PART FIRST

THE passage selected for quotation follows upon that scene where Prince Hal's practical jest upon Falstaff has expanded into Falstaff's famous history of his prowess against the 'men in buckram.' The imposture has been exposed. Falstaff has admitted that he did run away from his sham assailants—he is disconcerted, but not outwitted. He had his reason: he did so upon an instinct that told him it was the king's son who was attacking him. 'Why, thou knowest I am as valiant as Hercules; but beware instinct: the lion will not touch the true prince. Instinct is a great matter, I was a coward on instinct.' The boon companions are now again carousing at the Boar's Head. The scene which follows is a play within a play. Reading it critically one cannot but wonder at finding such breadth and fulness of humour never deviating into farce, at the excellence of the wit, and at the perfection of the stage-craft.

The Boar's Head Tavern in Eastcheap.
Prince HENRY, POINS, BARDOLPH, GADSHILL,
PETO, Hostess.
Enter FALSTAFF.

How now, my sweet creature of bombast! How long is 't ago, Jack, since thou sawest thine own knee?

Falstaff. My own knee! When I was about thy years, Hal, I was not an eagle's talon in the waist; I could have crept into any alderman's thumb-ring. A plague of sighing and grief! it blows a man up like a bladder. There's villanous news abroad: here was Sir John Bracy from your father: you must to the court in the morning. That same mad fellow of the north, Percy, and he of Wales, that gave Amaimon the bastinado . . . and swore the devil his true liegeman upon the cross of a Welsh hook—what a plague call you him?

Poins. O! Glendower.

Falstaff. Owen, Owen; the same; and his son-in-law Mortimer, and old Northumberland; and that sprightly Scot of Scots, Douglas, that runs o' horseback up a hill perpendicular.

Prince. He that rides at high speed and with his pistol kills a sparrow flying.

Falstaff. You have hit it.

Prince. So did he never the sparrow.

Falstaff. Well, that rascal hath good mettle in him; he will not run.

Prince. Why, what a rascal art thou then, to praise him so for running!

Falstaff. O' horseback, ye cuckoo! but afoot he will not budge a foot.

Prince. Yes, Jack, upon instinct.

Falstaff. I grant ye, upon instinct. Well, he is

there too, and one Mordake, and a thousand blue-caps more. Worcester is stolen away to-night; thy father's beard is turned white with the news: you may buy land now as cheap as stinking mackerel. . . . But tell me, Hal, art thou not horrible afeard? thou being heir apparent, could the world pick thee out three such enemies again as that fiend Douglas, that spirit Percy, and that devil Glendower? Art thou not horribly afraid? doth not thy blood thrill at it?

Prince. Not a whit, i' faith; I lack some of thy instinct.

Falstaff. Well, thou wilt be horribly chid to-morrow when thou comest to thy father: if thou love me, practise an answer.

Prince. Do thou stand for my father, and examine me upon the particulars of my life.

Falstaff. Shall I? content: this chair shall be my state, this dagger my sceptre, and this cushion my crown.

Prince. Thy state is taken for a joint-stool, thy golden sceptre for a leaden dagger, and thy precious rich crown for a pitiful bald crown!

Falstaff. Well, an the fire of grace be not quite out of thee, now shalt thou be moved. Give me a cup of sack to make mine eyes look red, that it may be thought I have wept; for I must speak in passion, and I will do it in King Cambyses' vein.

Prince. Well, here is my leg.

Falstaff. And here is my speech. Stand aside, nobility.

Hostess. O Jesu! this is excellent sport, i' faith.

Falstaff. Weep not, sweet queen, for trickling tears are vain.

Hostess. O, the father! how he holds his countenance.

Falstaff. For God's sake, lords, convey my tristful queen,

For tears do stop the flood-gates of her eyes.

Hostess. O Jesu! he doth it as like one of these harlotry players as ever I see.

Falstaff. Peace, good pint-pot! peace, good tickle-brain! Harry, I do not only marvel where thou spendest thy time, but also how thou art accompanied: for though the camomile, the more it is trodden on the faster it grows, yet youth, the more it is wasted the sooner it wears. That thou art my son, I have partly thy mother's word, partly my own opinion; but chiefly a villanous trick of thine eye and a foolish hanging of thy nether lip, that doth warrant me. If then thou be son to me, here lies the point; why, being son to me, art thou so pointed at? Shall the blessed sun of heaven prove a micher and eat blackberries? a question not to be asked. Shall the son of England prove a thief and take purses? a question to be asked. There is a thing, Harry, which thou hast often heard of, and it is known to many in our land by the name of pitch: this pitch, as ancient writers do report, doth defile; so doth the company thou keepest; for, Harry, now I do not speak to thee in drink but in tears, not in pleasure but in passion, not in words only, but in woes also. And yet there is a virtuous man whom I have often noted in thy company, but I know not his name.

Prince. What manner of man, an it like your majesty?

Falstaff. A goodly portly man, i' faith, and a corpulent; of a cheerful look, a pleasing eye, and a most noble carriage; and, as I think, his age some fifty, or, by 'r lady, inclining to threescore; and now I remember me, his name is Falstaff: if that man should be lewdly given, he deceiveth me; for, Harry, I see virtue in his looks. If then the tree may be known by the fruit, as the fruit by the tree, then, peremptorily I speak it, there is virtue in that Falstaff: him keep with, the rest banish. And tell me now, thou naughty varlet, tell me, where hast thou been this month?

Prince. Dost thou speak like a king? Do thou stand for me, and I 'll play my father.

Falstaff. Depose me? If thou dost it half so gravely, so majestically, both in word and matter, hang me up by the heels for a rabbit-sucker or a poulter's hare.

Prince. Well, here I am set.

Falstaff. And here I stand. Judge, my masters.

Prince. Now, Harry! whence come you?

Falstaff. My noble lord, from Eastcheap.

Prince. The complaints I hear of thee are grievous.

Falstaff. 'Sblood, my lord, they are false: nay, I'll tickle ye for a young prince, i' faith.

Prince. Swearest thou, ungracious boy? henceforth ne'er look on me. Thou art violently carried away from grace: there is a devil haunts thee in the likeness of an old fat man; a tun of man is thy companion. Why dost thou converse with that trunk of humours, that bolting-hutch of beastliness, that swoln parcel of dropsies, that hugh bombard of sack . . . that reverend vice, that grey iniquity, that father ruffian, that vanity in years? Wherein is he good but to taste sack and drink it? wherein neat and cleanly but to carve a capon and eat it? wherein cunning but in craft? wherein crafty but in villany? wherein villanous but in all things? wherein worthy but in nothing?

Falstaff. I would your grace would take me with you: whom means your grace?

Prince. That villanous abominable misleader of youth, Falstaff, that old white-bearded Satan.

Falstaff. My lord, the man I know.

Prince. I know thou dost.

Falstaff. But to say I know more harm in him than in myself were to say more than I know. That he is old, the more the pity, his white hairs do witness it: but that he is, saving your reverence, a whoremaster, that I utterly deny. If sack and sugar be a fault, God help the wicked! If to be old and merry be a sin, then many an old host that I know is damned: if to be fat be to be hated, then Pharaoh's lean kine are to be loved. No, my good lord; banish Peto, banish Bardolph, banish Poins; but for sweet Jack Falstaff, kind Jack Falstaff, true Jack Falstaff, valiant Jack Falstaff, and therefore more valiant, being, as he is, old Jack Falstaff, banish not him thy Harry's company, banish not him thy Harry's company: banish plump Jack, and banish all the world.

Prince. I do, I will.

BEN JONSON

BORN 1573.   DIED 1637.

BEN JONSON stands at the head of that school of dramatists who take for their *Dramatis Personæ* not individuals but conventional types, and who somewhat ignore the complexities of human nature. No argument is wanted to show that Shakspere's method of truly holding the mirror up to nature is the higher, the greater, and the truer method, but Jonson has ancient tradition in favour of his view of the dramatic art. Actors, authors, and audiences have always been in a conspiracy to accept the conventional types—the stock stage characters—as a saving of time, trouble, and imagination; and Molière himself, in his 'Misanthrope,' in 'L'Avare,' in 'L'École des Femmes,' and in 'Tartuffe,' ranges himself among the typists. The French playwright, however, by reason of his great dramatic genius, his inexhaustible fancy and fertility of resources, is continually carried beyond the region of mere typical representation. Not so with Ben Jonson, who seldom departs from the strict tradition: his cowardly braggarts are most inveterate cowards and braggarts, his knaves most arrant knaves, his fools have no redeeming touch of good sense, and his misers are grasping and avaricious beyond all human precedent and possibility. Nevertheless, the magnificent genius of the man—chiefly a literary genius—takes the reader's judgment by storm; and if the reader's, how much more would the hearer be captivated by the broad persistent humour of Bobadill and the mordant cynicism of Mosca and Volpone!

BEN JONSON

THE ALCHEMIST

LOVEWIT, a gentleman of middle age, 'wont to affect mirth and wit,' forsakes his London house on account of the Plague, leaving it in charge of Jeremy Face, his servant. Face falls in with Subtle, a charlatan and pretended seeker after the philosopher's stone, and Dol Common, his accomplice, who induce him to enter into partnership with them.

They take up their abode in Lovewit's house, and under pretence of practising alchemy and soothsaying draw thither a great number of dupes; among others Sir Epicure Mammon, with his friend Pertinax Surly (who, however, holds them to be impostors), Abel Drugger, a tobacconist, and Lady Pliant, a rich young widow.

The master of the house unexpectedly returning, the alchemist and his confederates are exposed, but Lovewit pardons Face's misconduct in consideration of his having brought him acquainted with Lady Pliant, whom he marries.

A Room in LOVEWIT'S *House.*

SUBTLE, *in his velvet cap and gown, followed by* ABEL DRUGGER.

Subtle. What is your name, say you, Abel Drugger?
Drugger. Yes, sir.

Subtle. A seller of tobacco?
Drugger. Yes, sir.
Subtle. Umph!
Free of the grocers?
Drugger. Ay, an't please you.
Subtle. Well—
Your business, Abel?
Drugger. This, an't please your worship;
I am a young beginner, and am building
Of a new shop, an't like your worship, just
At corner of a street :—Here is the plot on 't—
And I would know by art, sir, of your worship,
Which way I should make my door, by necromancy,
And where my shelves; and which should be for boxes,
And which for pots. I would be glad to thrive, sir:
And I was wish'd to your worship by a gentleman,
One Captain Face, that says you know men's planets,
And their good angels, and their bad.
Subtle. I do,
If I do see them—

Enter FACE.

Face. What! my honest Abel?
Thou art well met here.
Drugger. Troth, sir, I was speaking
Just as your worship came here, of your worship:
I pray you speak for me to master doctor.
Face. He shall do anything. Doctor, do you hear!

This is my friend, Abel, an honest fellow ;
He lets me have good tobacco, and he does not
Sophisticate it with sack-lees or oil,
Nor washes it in muscadel and grains,
Nor buries it in gravel underground,
Wrapp'd up in greasy leather, . . .
But keeps it in fine lily pots, that, open'd,
Smell like conserve of roses, or French beans.
He has his maple block, his silver tongs,
Winchester pipes, and fire of Jupiter :
A neat, spruce, honest fellow, and no goldsmith.
   Subtle. He is a fortunate fellow, that I am sure on.
   Face. Already, sir, have you found it? Lo thee, Abel !
   Subtle. And in right way toward riches—
   Face. Sir !
   Subtle. This summer
He will be of the clothing of his company,
And next spring call'd to the scarlet ; spend what he can.
   Face. What, and so little beard ?
   Subtle. Sir, you must think,
He may have a receipt to make hair come :
But he'll be wise, preserve his youth, and fine for 't ;
His fortune looks for him another way.
   Face. 'Slid, Doctor, how canst thou know this so
      soon ?
I am amused at that !
   Subtle. By a rule, captain,
In metoposcopy, which I do work by ;

A certain star in the forehead, which you see not.
Your chestnut or your olive colour'd face
Does never fail : and your long ear doth promise.
I knew 't by certain spots too in his teeth,
And on the nail of his mercurial finger.

Face. Which finger's that?

Subtle. His little finger. Look,
You were born upon a Wednesday?

Drugger. Yes, indeed, sir.

Subtle. The thumb, in chiromancy, we give Venus;
The forefinger, to Jove; the midst, to Saturn;
The ring, to Sol; the least, to Mercury,
Who was the lord of life, sir, of his horoscope,
His house of life being Libra; which fore-showed,
He should be a merchant, and should trade with balance.

Face. Why, this is strange? Is it not, honest Nab?

Subtle. There is a ship now coming from Ormus,
That shall yield him such a commodity
Of drugs—This is the west, and this is the south?

Pointing to the plan.

Drugger. Yes, sir.

Subtle. And those are your two sides?

Drugger. Ay, sir.

Subtle. And those are your two sides?

Drugger. Ay, sir.

Subtle. Make me your door, then, south; your broad
    side, west :
And on the east side of your shop, aloft,

Write Mathlai, Tarmiel, and Baraborat;
Upon the north part, Rael, Velel, Thiel.
They are the names of those mercurial spirits
That do fright flies from boxes.
 Drugger. Yes, sir.
 Subtle. And
Beneath your threshold, bury me a load-stone
To draw in gallants that wear spurs: the rest,
They'll seem to follow.
 Face. That's a secret, Nab!
 Subtle. And on your stall, a puppet, with a vice
And a court fucus to call city-dames:
You shall deal much with minerals.
 Drugger. Sir, I have
At home already—
 Subtle. Ay, I know you have arsenic,
Vitriol, sal-tartar, argaile, alkali,
Cinoper: I know all.—This fellow, captain,
Will come, in time, to be a great distiller,
And give a say—I will not say directly
But very fair—at the philosopher's stone.
 Face. Why, how now, Abel! is this true?
 Drugger. Aside to FACE. Good captain,
What must I give?
 Face. Nay, I'll not counsel thee.
Thou hear'st what wealth (he says, spend what thou
  canst,)
Thou'rt like to come to.

C

Drugger. I would gi' him a crown.

Face. A crown! and toward such a fortune? heart,
Thou shalt rather gi' him thy shop. No gold about
    thee?

Drugger. Yes, I have a portague, I have kept this
    half year.

Face. Out on thee, Nab! 'slight, there was such an
    offer—

Shalt keep 't no longer, I'll give 't him for thee. Doctor,
Nab prays your worship to drink this, and swears
He will appear more grateful, as your skill
Does raise him in the world.

Drugger. I would entreat
Another favour of his worship.

Face. What is 't, Nab?

Drugger. But to look over, sir, my almanack,
And cross out my ill days, that I may neither
Bargain, nor trust upon them.

Face. That he shall, Nab;
Leave it, it shall be done, 'gainst afternoon.

Subtle. And a direction for his shelves.

Face. Now, Nab,
Art thou well pleased, Nab?

Drugger. 'Thank, sir, both your worships.

Face. Away.—   *Exit* DRUGGER.

. . . .

        Enter DOL COMMON.

Subtle. . . . How now,

What says my dainty Dolkin?
  Dol. Yonder fish-wife
Will not away.   And there's your giantess.

  . . . .

  Subtle. Heart, I cannot speak with them.
  Dol. Not afore night, I have told them in a voice,
Thorough the trunk, like one of our familiars.
But I have spied Sir Epicure Mammon.—
  Subtle. Where?
  Dol. Coming along, at far end of the lane,
Slow of his feet, but earnest of his tongue
To one that's with him.
  Subtle. Face, go you and shift.   *Exit* FACE.
Dol, you must presently make ready, too.
  Dol. Why, what's the matter?
  Subtle. O, I did look for him
With the sun's rising: 'marvel he could sleep.
This is the day I am to perfect for him
The magisterium, our great work, the stone;
And yield it, made, into his hands: of which
He has, this month, talked as he were possess'd,
And now he's dealing pieces on 't away.—
Methinks I see him entering ordinaries
  . . . . and plaguy houses,
Reaching his dose, walking Moorfields for lepers
And offering citizens' wives pomander-bracelets
As his preservative, made of the elixir;
Searching the spittal, to make old bawds young;

And the highways, for beggars to make rich :
I see no end of his labours.   He will make
Nature ashamed of her long sleep : when art,
Who's but a step-dame, shall do more than she,
In her best love to mankind, ever could :
If his dream lasts, he 'll turn the age to gold.

                                            Exeunt.

        An Outer Room in LOVEWIT'S *House.*

    Enter Sir EPICURE MAMMON *and* SURLY.

  Mammon. Come on, sir.   Now you set your foot on shore
In *Novo Orbe;* here's the rich Peru :
And there within, sir, are the golden mines,
Great Solomon's Ophir !   He was sailing to 't,
Three years, but we have reach'd it in ten months.
This is the day, wherein, to all my friends,
I will pronounce the happy word, BE RICH ;
THIS DAY YOU SHALL BE SPECTATISSIMI.
You shall no more deal with the hollow dye
Or the frail card. . . .   No more
Shall thirst of satin, or the covetous hunger
Of velvet entrails for a rude-spun cloke,
To be displayed at Madam Augusta's, make
The sons of Sword and Hazard fall before
The golden calf, and on their knees, whole nights,
Commit idolatry with wine and trumpets :
Or go a feasting after drum and ensign.

No more of this. . . . .
And unto thee I speak it first, BE RICH.
Where is my Subtle, there? Within, ho!
   Face. Within. Sir, he 'll come to you by and by.
   Mammon. That is his fire-drake,
His Lungs, his Zephyrus, he that puffs his coals,
Till he firk nature up, in her own centre.
You are not faithful, sir. This night, I 'll change
All that is metal, in my house, to gold:
And early in the morning will I send
To all the plumbers and the pewterers,
And buy their tin and lead up; and to Lothbury
For all the copper.
   Surly. What, and turn that too?
   Mammon. Yes, and I 'll purchase Devonshire and
      Cornwall,
And make the perfect Indies. You admire now?
   Surly. No, faith.
   Mammon. But when you see th' effects of the Great
      Medicine,
Of which one part projected on a hundred
Of Mercury, or Venus, or the moon,
Shall turn it to as many of the sun;
Nay, to a thousand; so ad infinitum:
You will believe me.
   Surly. Yes, when I see 't, I will.

     . . . .
   Mammon. Ha! why?

Do you think I fable with you? I assure you,
He that has once the flower of the sun,
The perfect ruby, which we call elixir,
Not only can do that, but, by its virtue,
Can confer honour, love, respect, long life;
Give safety, valour, yea, and victory,
To whom he will. In eight and twenty days,
I'll make an old man of fourscore, a child.
   Surly. No doubt he's that already.
   Mammon. Nay, I mean,
Restore his years, renew him, like an eagle,
To the fifth age; make him get sons and daughters,
Young giants; as our philosophers have done,
The ancient patriarchs, afore the flood,
By taking, once a week, on a knife's point,
The quantity of a grain of mustard of it,
Become stout Marses and beget young Cupids.
  . . . . . 'Tis the secret
Of nature naturized 'gainst all infections,
Cures all diseases coming of all causes,
A month's grief in a day, a year's in twelve;
And, of what age soever, in a month:
Past all the doses of your drugging doctors.
I'll undertake, withal, to fright the plague
Out of the kingdom in three months.
   Surly. And I'll
Be bound, the players shall sing your praises, there,
Without their poets.

Mammon. Sir, I'll do't. Mean time,
I'll give away so much unto my man,
Shall serve the whole city, with preservative,
Weekly; each house his dose, and at the rate—
  Surly. As he that built the Water-work, does with
    water?
Mammon. You are incredulous.
Surly. Faith, I have a humour,
I would not willingly be gull'd. Your stone
Cannot transmute me.
Mammon. Pertinax, [my] Surly,
Will you believe antiquity? records?
I'll show you a book where Moses and his sister,
And Solomon have written of the art;
Ay, and a treatise penned by Adam—
  Surly. How!
Mammon. Of the philosopher's stone, and in High
    Dutch.
  Surly. Did Adam write, sir, in High Dutch?
Mammon. He did;
Which proves it was the primitive tongue.
  Surly. What paper?
Mammon. On cedar board.
  Surly. O, that, indeed, they say,
Will last 'gainst worms.
  Mammon. 'Tis like your Irish wood,
'Gainst cob-webs. I have a piece of Jason's fleece, too,
Which was no other than a book of alchemy,

Writ in large sheep-skin, a good fat ram-vellum.
Such was Pythagoras' thigh, Pandora's tub,
And, all that fable of Medea's charms,
The manner of our work; the bulls, our furnace,
Still breathing fire; our argent-vive, the dragon:
The dragon's teeth, mercury sublimate,
That keeps the whiteness, hardness, and the biting;
And they are gather'd into Jason's helm,
The alembic, and then sow'd in Mars his field,
And thence sublimed so often, till they're fixed.
Both this, the Hesperian garden, Cadmus' story,
Jove's shower, the boon of Midas, Argus' eyes,
Boccace his Demogorgon, thousands more,
All abstract riddles of our stone.

Enter FACE, as a Servant.

How now!
Do we succeed? Is our day come? and holds it?
　Face. The evening will set red upon you, sir;
You have colour for it, crimson: the red ferment
Has done his office; three hours hence prepare you
To see projection.
　Mammon. Pertinax, my Surly,
Again I say to thee, aloud, Be rich.
This day, thou shalt have ingots; and, to-morrow,
Give lords th' affront. . . . .
. . . . My only care is
Where to get stuff enough now, to project on;

This town will not half serve me.

Face. No, sir! buy
The covering off o' churches.

Mammon. That's true.

Face. Yes.
Let them stand bare, as do their auditory;
Or cap them, new, with shingles.

Mammon. No, good thatch:
Thatch will lie light upon the rafters, Lungs.—
Lungs, I will manumit thee from the furnace;
I will restore thee thy complexion, Puffe,
Lost in the embers; and repair this brain,
Hurt with the fume o' the metals.

Face. I have blown, sir,
Hard for your worship; thrown by many a coal
When 'twas not beech; weigh'd those I put in, just,
To keep your heat still even; these blear'd eyes
Have wak'd to read your several colours, sir,
Of the pale citron, the green lion, the crow,
The peacock's tail, the plumed swan.

Mammon. And, lastly,
Thou has descry'd the flower, the *sanguis agni?*

Face. Yes, sir.

Mammon. Where's master?

Face. At his prayers, sir, he;
Good man, he's doing his devotions
For the success.

Mammon. Lungs, I will set a period

To all thy labours; thou shalt be the master
Of my seraglio. . . . .
Thou art sure thou saw'st it blood?
 Face. Both blood and spirit, sir.
 Mammon. I will have all my beds blown up, not stuft:
Down is too hard: and then, mine oval room
Fill'd with such pictures as Tiberius took
From Elephantis, and dull Aretine
But coldly imitated. . . . . My mists
I'll have of perfume, vapour'd 'bout the room,
To lose ourselves in; and my baths, like pits
To fall into; from whence we will come forth,
And roll us dry in gossamer and roses.
Is it arrived at ruby? . . . .
 . . . . And my flatterers
Shall be the pure and gravest of divines,
That I can get for money. My mere fools,
 Eloquent burgesses. . . . .
We will be brave, Puffe, now we have the med'cine.
My meat shall all come in, in Indian shells,
Dishes of agate set in gold, and studded
With emeralds, sapphires, hyacinths, and rubies.
The tongues of carps, dormice, and camels' heels,
Boil'd in the spirit of sol, and dissolv'd pearl,
Apicius' diet 'gainst the epilepsy:
And I will eat these broths with spoons of amber,
Headed with diamond and carbuncle.
My foot-boy shall eat pheasants, calver'd salmons,

Knots, godwits, lampreys : I myself will have
The beards of barbels served, instead of sallads ;`
Oil'd mushrooms ; and the swelling unctuous paps
Of a fat pregnant sow, newly cut off,
Drest with an exquisite and poignant sauce ;
For which, I'll say unto my cook, *There's gold,
Go forth, and be a knight.*
    Face. Sir, I'll go look
A little, how it heightens.   *Exit.*
    Mammon. Do.—My shirts
I'll have of taffeta-sarsnet, soft and light
As cobwebs ; and for all my other raiment,
It shall be such as might provoke the Persian,
Were he to teach the world riot anew.
My gloves of fishes and birds' skins perfumed
With gums of paradise and eastern air—
    Surly. And do you think to have the stone with
    this ?
    Mammon. No, I do think t' have all this with the
    stone.
    Surly. Why, I have heard, he must be *homo frugi*,
A pious, holy, and religious man,
One free from mortal sin, a very virgin.
    Mammon. That makes it, sir ; he is so : but I
    buy it ;
My venture brings it me. He, honest wretch,
A notable, superstitious, good soul,
Hath worn his knees bare, and his slippers bald,

With prayer and fasting for it: and, sir, let him
Do it alone, for me, still.   Here he comes.
Not a profane word afore him: 'tis poison.

THE FOX

THIS play derives its name from the cunning devices of Volpone. Assuming the character of a wealthy old man, childless, and at the point of death, he, by giving hopes of making them his heirs, obtains rich gifts from Voltore, an advocate, Corbaccio, and many more, whose generosity is stimulated by the golden prospects artfully held out to them by Mosca, Volpone's parasite and confederate. To make sport of them, Volpone orders Mosca to spread a report that he is dead, and has left all his wealth to Mosca.

After witnessing, unseen, the discomfiture of the disappointed heirs, who assemble at his house, Volpone disguises himself and follows them, to taunt them further. Mosca meanwhile, taking advantage of the feigned death of his patron, takes possession of his estate and denounces Volpone as an impostor. Finally both are unmasked and brought to justice.

Sir Politick Would-be is a credulous, foolish knight, whose foibles are played upon by Peregrine, a gentleman on his travels.

A Room in VOLPONE'S *House.*

VOLPONE, MOSCA.   (*Knocking without.*)

Volpone. Who's that? Look, Mosca!

Mosca. 'Tis Signior Voltore, the advocate;
I know him by his knock.

Volpone. Fetch me my gown,
My furs and night-caps; say, my couch is changing,
And let him entertain himself awhile
Without i' the gallery.   *Exit* MOSCA.
              Now, now, my clients
Begin their visitation! Vulture, kite,
Raven, and gorcrow, all my birds of prey,
That think me turning carcase, now they come;
I am not for them yet—

    Re-enter MOSCA, *with the gown, etc.*

              How now! The news?
Mosca. A piece of plate, sir.
Volpone. Of what bigness?
Mosca. Huge,
Massy and antique, with your name inscribed,
And arms engraven.
Volpone. Good! and not a fox
Stretched on the earth, with fine delusive sleights,
Mocking a gaping crow? ha, Mosca!
Mosca. Sharp, sir.
Volpone. Give me my furs.   *Puts on his sick dress.*
Why dost thou laugh so, man?
Mosca. I cannot choose, sir, when I apprehend
What thoughts he has without now, as he walks:
That this might be the last gift he should give;
This, this would fetch you; if you died to-day,
And gave him all, what should he do to-morrow;

What large return would come of all his ventures;
How he should worshipp'd be, and reverenced;
Ride with his furs, and foot-cloths; waited on
By herds of fools and clients; have clear way
Made for his mule, as lettered as himself;
Be called the great and learned advocate:
And then concludes, there's nought impossible.

Volpone. Yes, to be learned, Mosca.

Mosca. O, no: rich
Implies it. Hood an ass with reverend purple,
So you can hide his two ambitious ears,
And he shall pass for a cathedral doctor.

Volpone. My caps, my caps, good Mosca. Fetch him in.

Mosca. Stay, sir; your ointment for your eyes.

Volpone. That's true;
Dispatch, dispatch: I long to have possession
Of my new present.

Mosca. That, and thousands more
I hope to see you lord of.

Volpone. Thanks, kind Mosca.

Mosca. And that, when I am lost in blended dust,
And hundred such as I am, in succession—

Volpone. Nay, that were too much, Mosca.

Mosca. You shall live,
Still, to delude these harpies.

Volpone. Loving Mosca!
'Tis well: my pillow now, and let him enter.

Exit MOSCA.

Now, my feign'd cough, my phthisic and my gout,
My apoplexy, palsy, and catarrhs,
Help, with your forced functions, this my posture,
Wherein, this three year, I have milked their hopes.
He comes; I hear him—Uh! *Coughing.* uh! uh!
uh! O—

Re-enter MOSCA, introducing VOLTORE, with a piece of plate.

MOSCA. *To VOLTORE.* You still are what you were,
sir. Only you
Of all the rest, are he commands his love,
And you do wisely to preserve it thus,
With early visitation, and kind notes
Of your good meaning to him, which, I know,
Cannot but come most grateful. Patron! sir!
Here's Signior Voltore is come.

Volpone. Faintly. What say you?

Mosca. Sir, Signior Voltore is come this morning
To visit you.

Volpone. I thank him.

Mosca. And hath brought
A piece of antique plate, bought of St. Mark,
With which he here presents you.

Volpone. He is welcome.
Pray him to come more often.

Mosca. Yes.

Voltore. What says he?

Mosca. He thanks you, and desires you see him often.
Volpone. Mosca.
Mosca. My patron!
Volpone. Bring him near, where is he?
I long to feel his hand.
Mosca. The plate is here, sir.
Voltore. How fare you, sir?
Volpone. I thank you, Signior Voltore;
Where is the plate? mine eyes are bad.
Voltore. Putting it into his hands. I'm sorry
To see you still thus weak.
Mosca. Aside. That he's not weaker.
Volpone. You are too munificent.
Voltore. No, sir; would to heaven,
I could as well give health to you as that plate!
Volpone. You give, sir, what you can : I thank you.
Your love
Hath taste in this, and shall not be unanswered:
I pray you see me often.
Voltore. Yes, I shall, sir.
Volpone. Be not far from me.
Mosca. Do you observe that, sir?
Volpone. Hearken unto me still; it will concern you.
Mosca. You are a happy man, sir; know your good.
Volpone. I cannot now last long—
Mosca. You are his heir, sir.
Voltore. Am I?
Volpone. I feel me going; Uh! uh! uh! uh!

I'm sailing to my port. Uh! uh! uh! uh!
And I am glad I am so near my haven.
   Mosca. Alas, kind gentleman! Well, we must all
      go—
   Voltore. But, Mosca—
   Mosca. Age will conquer.
   Voltore. Pray thee, hear me:
Am I inscribed his heir for certain?
   Mosca. Are you!
I do beseech you, sir, you will vouchsafe
To write me in your family. All my hopes
Depend upon your worship: I am lost,
Except the rising sun do shine on me.
   Voltore. It shall both shine, and warm thee, Mosca.
   Mosca. Sir,
I am a man, that hath not done your love
All the worst offices: here I wear your keys,
See all your coffers and your caskets lock'd,
Keep the poor inventory of your jewels,
Your plate and monies; am your steward, sir,
Husband your goods here.
   Voltore. But am I sole heir?
   Mosca. Without a partner, sir; confirm'd this morn-
      ing:
The wax is warm yet, and the ink scarce dry
Upon the parchment.
   Voltore. Happy, happy me!
By what good chance, sweet Mosca?

Mosca. Your desert, sir;
I know no second cause.
    Voltore. Thy modesty
Is not to know it; well, we shall requite it.
    Mosca. He ever liked your course, sir; that first
        took him,
I oft have heard him say, how he admired
Men of your large profession, that could speak
To every cause, and things mere contraries,
Till they were hoarse again, yet all be law;
That, with most quick agility, could turn
And re-turn; could make knots, and undo them;
Give forked counsel; take provoking gold
In either hand, and put it up: these men,
He knew would thrive with their humility.
And, for his part, he thought he should be blest
To have his heir of such a suffering spirit,
So wise, so grave, of so perplexed a tongue,
And loud withal, that would not wag, nor scarce
Lie still, without a fee; when every word
Your worship but lets fall, is a chequin!
                          Knocking without.
Who's that? one knocks; I would not have you seen,
    sir.
And yet—pretend you came, and went in haste:
I'll fashion an excuse—and, gentle sir,
When you do come to swim in golden lard,
Up to the arms in honey, that your chin

Is borne up stiff, with fatness of the flood,
Think on your vassal ; but remember me :
I have not been your worst of clients.
   Voltore. Mosca !—
   Mosca. When will you have your inventory brought,
     sir?
Or see a copy of the will ?—Anon !—
I 'll bring them to you, sir.   Away, be gone,
Put business in your face.   *Exit VOLTORE.*
   Volpone. Springing up. Excellent Mosca ! Come
     hither, let me kiss thee.
   Mosca. Keep you still, sir.
Here is Corbaccio.
   Volpone. Set the plate away :
The vulture's gone, and the old raven's come.
   Mosca. Betake you to your silence and your sleep.
              Putting the plate to the rest.
Stand there and multiply.   Now, we shall see
A wretch who is indeed more impotent
Than this can feign to be ; yet hopes to hop
Over his grave—

         Enter CORBACCIO.

       Signior Corbaccio !
You 're very welcome, sir.

St. Mark's Place; a retired corner before CORVINO'S *House.*

Enter Sir POLITICK WOULD-BE *and* PEREGRINE.

Sir Politick. Sir, to a wise man, all the world's his soil:
It is not Italy, nor France, nor Europe,
That must bound me, if my fates call me forth.
Yet, I protest, it is no salt desire
Of seeing countries, shifting a religion,
Nor any disaffection to the state
Where I was bred, and unto which I owe
My dearest plots, hath brought me out; much less,
That idle, antique, stale, grey-headed project
Of knowing men's minds and manners, with Ulysses!
But a peculiar humour of my wife's
Laid for this height of Venice, to observe,
To quote, to learn the language, and so forth—
I hope you travel, sir, with license?
   Peregrine. Yes.
   Sir Politick. I dare the safelier converse—How long, sir,
Since you left England?
   Peregrine. Seven weeks.
   Sir Politick. So lately!
You have not been with my lord ambassador?
   Peregrine. Not yet, sir.

Sir Politick. Pray you, what news, sir, vents our climate?
I heard last night a most strange thing reported
By some of my lord's followers, and I long
To hear how 'twill be seconded.
Peregrine. What was't, sir?
Sir Politick. Marry, sir, of a raven that should build
In a ship royal of the king's.
Peregrine. Aside. This fellow,
Does he gull me, trow? or is gulled?
Your name, sir.
Sir Politick. My name is Politick Would-be.
Peregrine. Aside. O, that speaks him.—
A knight, sir?
Sir Politick. A poor knight, sir.
Peregrine. Your lady,
Lies here in Venice, for intelligence
Of tires, and fashions, and behaviour,
Among the courtezans? the fine Lady Would-be?
Sir Politick. Yes, sir; the spider and the bee ofttimes,
Suck from one flower.
Peregrine. Good Sir Politick,
I cry you mercy; I have heard much of you:
'Tis true, sir, of your raven.
Sir Politick. On your knowledge?
Peregrine. Yes, and your lion's whelping in the Tower.
Sir Politick. Another whelp!
Peregrine. Another, sir.

Sir Politick. Now, heaven!
What prodigies be these? The fires at Berwick!
And the new star! these things concurring, strange,
And full of omen! Saw you those meteors?

Peregrine. I did, sir.

Sir Politick. Fearful! Pray you, sir, confirm me,
Were there three porpoises seen above the bridge,
As they give out?

Peregrine. Six, and a sturgeon, sir.

Sir Politick. I am astonish'd.

Peregrine. Nay, sir, be not so;
I'll tell you a greater prodigy than these.

Sir Politick. What should these things portend?

Peregrine. The very day
(Let me be sure) that I put forth from London,
There was a whale discovered in the river,
As high as Woolwich, that had waited there,
Few know how many months, for the subversion
Of the Stode fleet.

Sir Politick. Is't possible? believe it,
'Twas either sent from Spain, or the archdukes:
Spinola's whale, upon my life, my credit!
Will they not leave these projects? Worthy sir,
Some other news.

Peregrine. Faith, Stone the fool is dead,
And they do lack a tavern fool extremely.

Sir Politick. Is Mass Stone dead?

Peregrine. He's dead, sir; why, I hope

You thought him not immortal. *Aside.* O, this knight,
Were he well known, would be a precious thing
To fit our English stage: he that should write
But such a fellow, should be thought to feign
Extremely, if not maliciously.
   Sir Politick. Stone dead!
   Peregrine. Dead.—Lord! how deeply, sir, you apprehend it?
He was no kinsman to you?
   Sir Politick. That I know of.
Well! that same fellow was an unknown fool.
   Peregrine. And yet you knew him, it seems?
   Sir Politick. I did so. Sir,
I knew him one of the most dangerous heads
Living within the state, and so I held him.
   Peregrine. Indeed, sir?
   Sir Politick. While he lived, in action.
He has received weekly intelligence,
Upon my knowledge, out of the Low Countries,
For all parts of the world, in cabbages;
And those dispensed again to ambassadors,
In oranges, musk-melons, apricocks,
Lemons, pome-citrons and such-like; sometimes
In Colchester oysters and your Selsey cockles.
   Peregrine. You make me wonder.
   Sir Politick. Sir, upon my knowledge.
Nay, I've observed him, at your public ordinary,
Take his advertisement from a traveller,

A conceal'd statesman, in a trencher of meat;
And instantly, before the meal was done,
Convey an answer in a tooth-pick.

Peregrine. Strange!
How could this be, sir?

Sir Politick. Why, the meat was cut
So like his character, and so laid, as he
Must easily read the cipher.

Peregrine. I have heard,
He could not read, sir.

Sir Politick. So 'twas given out,
In policy, by those that did employ him;
But he could read, and had your languages,
And to 't, as sound a noddle—

Peregrine. I have heard, sir,
That your baboons were spies, and that they were
A kind of subtle nation near to China.

Sir Politick. Ay, ay, your Mamaluchi. Faith they had
Their hand in a French plot or two; but they
Were so extremely given to women, as
They made discovery of all: yet I
Had my advices here, on Wednesday last,
From one of their own coat, they were return'd,
Made their relations, as the fashion is,
And now stand fair for fresh employment.

Peregrine. Aside. 'Heart!
This Sir Pol will be ignorant of nothing.—
It seems, sir, you know all.

Sir Politick. Not all, sir, but
I have some general notions. I do love
To note and to observe : though I live out,
Free from the active torrent, yet I'd mark
The currents and the passages of things,
For mine own private use ; and know the ebbs
And flows of state.
    Peregrine. Believe it, sir, I hold
Myself in no small tie unto my fortunes,
For casting me thus luckily upon you,
Whose knowledge, if your bounty equal it,
May do me great assistance, in instruction
For my behaviour, and my bearing, which
Is yet so rude and raw.
    Sir Politick. Why, came you forth
Empty of rules for travel ?
    Peregrine. Faith, I had
Some common ones, from out that vulgar grammar,
Which he that cried Italian to me, taught me.
    Sir Politick. Why this it is which spoils all our brave bloods,
Trusting our hopeful gentry unto pedants,
Fellows of outside, and mere bark. You seem
To be a gentleman, of ingenuous race :—
I not profess it, but my fate hath been
To be, where I have been consulted with,
In this high kind, touching some great men's sons,
Persons of blood and honour.

EVERY MAN IN HIS HUMOUR

OLD Knowell is the father of Edward Knowell, a studious youth, and uncle of Master Stephen, a stupid, ill-conditioned country bumpkin. Stephen takes offence at a servant who brings a letter for Edward Knowell from Wellbred, his friend. Old Knowell opens this letter, which contains an invitation to a merry-making and some ridicule of himself. Fearing that his son has fallen into bad company, he resolves to follow him.

Edward Knowell, Wellbred, and Stephen (who is the butt of the others), come across Captain Bobadill, a braggart and coward, and Master Matthew, a town fool, as Stephen is a country fool. The young men go to the house of Kitely, a merchant, where Wellbred, who is Kitely's wife's brother, frequently entertains his friends, to the annoyance of Kitely, he being a prey to jealousy. Meanwhile Brainworm, servant to Old Knowell, assumes the disguise of an old soldier, in the interests of Edward Knowell, to prevent his father from meeting him, and afterwards in various other disguises causes many complications and misunderstandings, which are finally all cleared up at the house of Justice Clement, 'an old, merry magistrate.'

A Room in KNOWELL'S *House.*

Enter E. KNOWELL *with a letter in his hand, followed by* BRAINWORM.

E. Knowell. Did he open it, say'st thou?

Brainworm. Yes, o' my word, sir, and read the contents.

E. Knowell. That scarce contents me. What

countenance, prithee, made he in the reading of it? Was he angry, or pleased?

Brainworm. Nay, sir, I saw him not read it, nor open it, I assure your worship.

E. Knowell. No! how know'st thou then that he did either?

Brainworm. Marry, sir, because he charged me, on my life, to tell nobody that he opened it; which, unless he had done, he would never fear to have it revealed.

E. Knowell. That's true: well, I thank thee, Brainworm.

Enter STEPHEN.

Stephen. O, Brainworm, didst thou not see a fellow here in what-sha-call-him doublet? he brought mine uncle a letter e'en now.

Brainworm. Yes, Master Stephen, what of him?

Stephen. O, I have such a mind to beat him—where is he, canst thou tell?

Brainworm. Faith, he is not of that mind: he is gone, Master Stephen.

Stephen. Gone! which way? when went he? how long since?

Brainworm. He is rid hence; he took horse at the street-door.

Stephen. And I staid in the fields! . . . Scanderbag rogue! O that I had but a horse to fetch him back again!

Brainworm. Why, you may have my master's gelding, to save your longing, sir.

Stephen. But I have no boots, that's the spite on 't.

Brainworm. Why, a fine wisp of hay, roll'd hard, Master Stephen.

Stephen. No, faith, it's no boot to follow him now: let him e'en go and hang. Prithee, help me to truss me a little: he does so vex me—

Brainworm. You'll be worse vexed when you are trussed, Master Stephen. Best keep unbraced, and walk yourself till you be cold; your choler may founder you else.

Stephen. By my faith, and so I will, now thou tell'st me on 't: how dost thou like my leg, Brainworm?

Brainworm. A very good leg, Master Stephen; but the woollen stocking does not commend it so well.

Stephen. Foh! the stockings be good enough, now summer is coming on, for the dust: I'll have a pair of silk against winter, that I go to dwell in the town. I think my leg would show in a silk hose.

Brainworm. Believe me, Master Stephen, rarely well.

Stephen. In sadness, I think it would: I have a reasonable good leg.

Brainworm. You have an excellent good leg, Master Stephen; but I cannot stay to praise it any longer now, and I am very sorry for it. *Exit.*

Stephen. Another time will serve, Brainworm. Gramercy for this.

E. Knowell. Ha, ha, ha!

Stephen. 'Slid, I hope he laughs not at me; an he do—

E. Knowell. Here was a letter indeed, to be intercepted by a man's father, and do him good with him! He cannot but think most virtuously of me, and the sender, sure, that make the careful costermonger of him in our familiar epistles. Well, if he read this with patience, I'll troll ballads for Master John Trundle yonder, the rest of my mortality. It is true, and likely, my father may have as much patience as another man, for he takes much physic; and oft taking physic makes a man very patient. But would your packet, Master Wellbred, had arrived at him in such a minute of his patience! then had we known the end of it, which is now doubtful, and threatens. *Sees Master* STEPHEN. What, my wise cousin! nay, then I'll furnish our feast with one gull more towards the mess. He writes to me of a brace, and here's one, that's three; oh, for a fourth, Fortune, if ever thou'lt use thine eyes, I entreat thee—

Stephen. Oh, now I see who he laughed at: he laughed at somebody in that letter. By this good light, an he had laughed at me—

E. Knowell. How now, cousin Stephen, melancholy?

Stephen. Yes, a little : I thought you had laughed at me, cousin.

E. Knowell. Why, what an I had, coz? what would you have done?

Stephen. By this light, I would have told mine uncle.

E. Knowell. Nay, if you would have told your uncle, I did laugh at you, coz.

Stephen. Did you indeed?

E. Knowell. Yes, indeed.

Stephen. Why then—

E. Knowell. What then?

Stephen. I am satisfied; it is sufficient.

E. Knowell. Why, be it so, gentle coz.

. . . .

The Old Jewry. A Room in the Windmill Tavern.

Master MATTHEW, WELLBRED, and BOBADILL;
E. KNOWELL and Master STEPHEN.

Wellbred. Well, Captain Bobadill, master Matthew, pray you know this gentleman here; he is a friend of mine, and one that will deserve your affection. I know not your name, sir, *To STEPHEN.* but I shall be glad of any occasion to render me more familiar to you.

Stephen. My name is master Stephen, sir; I am this gentleman's own cousin, his father is mine uncle, sir : I am somewhat melancholy, but you shall command me, sir, in whatsoever is incident to a gentleman.

Bobadill. Sir, I must tell you this, I am no general man; but for master Wellbred's sake (you may embrace it at what height of favour you please,) I do communicate with you, and conceive you to be a gentleman of some parts; I love few words.

E. Knowell. And I fewer, sir; I have scarce enough to thank you.

Matthew. But are you, indeed, sir, so given to it?

Stephen. Ay, truly, sir, I am mightily given to melancholy.

Matthew. Oh, it's your only fine humour, sir; your true melancholy breeds your perfect fine wit, sir. I am melancholy myself, divers times, sir, and then do I no more but take pen and paper, presently, and overflow you half a score, or a dozen of sonnets at a sitting.

E. Knowell. Aside. Sure he utters them then by the gross.

Stephen. Truly, sir, and I love such things out of measure.

E. Knowell. I' faith, better than in measure, I'll undertake.

Matthew. Why, I pray you, sir, make use of my study, it's at your service.

Stephen. I thank you, sir, I shall be bold I warrant you; have you a stool there to be melancholy upon?

Matthew. That I have, sir, and some papers there of mine own doing, at idle hours, that you'll say there's some sparks of wit in 'em when you see them.

Wellbred. Aside. Would the sparks would kindle once, and become a fire amongst them! I might see self-love burnt for her heresy.

Stephen. Cousin, is it well? am I melancholy enough?

E. Knowell. Oh ay, excellent.

Wellbred. Captain Bobadill, why muse you so?

E. Knowell. He is melancholy too.

Bobadill. Faith, sir, I was thinking of a most honourable piece of service, was performed to-morrow, being St. Mark's day, shall be some ten years now.

E. Knowell. In what place, captain?

Bobadill. Why, at the beleaguering of Strigonium, where, in less than two hours, seven hundred resolute gentlemen, as any were in Europe, lost their lives upon the breach. I'll tell you, gentlemen, it was the first, but the best leaguer that ever I beheld with these eyes, except the taking in of—what do you call it? last year, by the Genoways; but that, of all other, was the most fatal and dangerous exploit that ever I was ranged in, since I first bore arms before the face of the enemy, as I am a gentleman and a soldier!

Stephen. So! I had as lief as an angel I could swear as well as that gentleman.

E. Knowell. Then, you were a servitor at both, it seems; at Strigonium, and what do you call 't?

Bobadill. O lord, sir! By St. George, I was the

first man that entered the breach; and had I not effected it with resolution, I had been slain if I had had a million of lives.

E. Knowell. 'Twas pity you had not ten; a cat's and your own, i' faith. But, was it possible?

Matthew. Pray you mark this discourse, sir.

Stephen. So I do.

Bobadill. I assure you, upon my reputation, 'tis true, and yourself shall confess.

E. Knowell. Aside.. You must bring me to the rack, first.

Bobadill. Observe me judicially, sweet sir; they had planted me three demi-culverins just in the mouth of the breach; now, sir, as we were to give on, their master-gunner (a man of no mean skill and mark, you must think), confronts me with his linstock, ready to give fire; I, spying his intendment, discharged my petronel in his bosom, and with these single arms, my poor rapier, ran violently upon the Moors that guarded the ordnance, and put 'em pell-mell to the sword.

Wellbred. To the sword! to the rapier, captain.

E. Knowell. Oh, it was a good figure observed, sir: but did you all this, captain, without hurting your blade?

Bobadill. Without any impeach o' the earth: you shall perceive, sir. *Shows his rapier.* It is the most fortunate weapon that ever rid on poor gentleman's thigh. Shall I tell you, sir? You talk of Morglay, Excalibur, Durindana, or so; tut! I lend no credit to

E

that is fabled of 'em : I know the virtue of mine own : and therefore I dare the boldlier maintain it.

Stephen. I marvel whether it be a Toledo or no.

Bobadill. A most perfect Toledo, I assure you, sir.

Stephen. I have a countryman of his here.

Matthew. Pray you, let's see, sir; yes, faith, it is.

Bobadill. This a Toledo ! Pish !

Stephen. Why do you pish, captain?

Bobadill. A Fleming, by heaven ! I'll buy them for a guilder apiece an I would have a thousand of them.

Moorfields.

Enter MATTHEW, E. KNOWELL, BOBADILL, and STEPHEN.

Matthew. Sir, did your eyes ever taste the like clown of him where we were to-day, Mr. Wellbred's half-brother? I think the whole earth cannot shew his parallel, by this daylight.

E. Knowell. We were now speaking of him: Captain Bobadill tells me he is fallen foul of you too.

Matthew. O, ay, sir, he threatened me with the bastinado.

Bobadill. Ay, but I think, I taught you prevention this morning, for that : you shall kill him beyond question ; if you be so generously minded.

Matthew. Indeed, it is a most excellent trick.

Fences.

Bobadill. O, you do not give spirit enough to your motion, you are too tardy, too heavy! O, it must be done like lightning, hay!

Practises at a post with his cudgel.

Matthew. Rare, captain!

Bobadill. Tut! 'tis nothing, an't be not done in a—punto.

E. Knowell. Captain, did you ever prove yourself upon any of our masters of defence here?

Matthew. O good sir! yes, I hope he has.

Bobadill. I will tell you, sir. Upon my first coming to the city, after my long travel for knowledge, in that mystery only, there came three or four of them to me, at a gentleman's house, where it was my chance to be resident at that time, to intreat my presence at their schools: and withal so much importuned me, that I protest to you, as I am a gentleman, I was ashamed of their rude demeanour out of all measure: Well, I told them that to come to a public school, they should pardon me, it was opposite, in diameter, to my humour; but if so be they would give their attendance at my lodging, I protested to do them what right or favour I could, as I was a gentleman, and so forth.

E. Knowell. So, sir! then you tried their skill?

Bobadill. Alas, soon tried: you shall hear, sir. Within two or three days after, they came; and, by honesty, fair sir, believe me, I graced them exceedingly, shewed them some two or three tricks of prevention have purchased them since a credit of admiration: they cannot deny this: and yet now they hate me, and why? because I am excellent; and for no other vile reason on the earth.

E. Knowell. This is strange and barbarous as ever I heard.

Bobadill. Nay, for a more instance of their preposterous natures; but note, sir. They have assaulted me, some three, four, five, six of them together, as I have walked alone in divers skirts i' the town, as Turnbull, Whitechapel, Shoreditch, which were then my quarters; and since, upon the Exchange, at my lodging, and at my ordinary: where I have driven them afore me the whole length of a street, in the open view of all our gallants, pitying to hurt them, believe me. Yet all this lenity will not overcome their spleen; they will be doing with the pismire, raising a hill a man may spurn abroad with his foot at pleasure. By myself, I could have slain them all, but I delight not in murder. I am loth to bear any other than this bastinado for them; yet I hold it good polity not to go disarmed, for though I be skilful, I may be oppressed with multitudes.

E. Knowell. Ay, believe me, may you, sir: and in my conceit, our whole nation should sustain the loss by it, if it were so.

Bobadill. Alas, no! what's a peculiar man to a nation? not seen.

E. Knowell. O, but your skill, sir.

Bobadill. Indeed, that might be some loss; but who respects it? I will tell you, sir, by the way of private and under seal; I am a gentleman, and live here obscure, and to myself; but were I known to her majesty and the lords,—observe me,—I would undertake, upon this poor head and life, for the public benefit of the state, not only to spare the entire lives of her subjects in general; but to save the one half, nay, three parts of her yearly charge in holding war, and against what enemy soever. And how would I do it, think you?

E. Knowell. Nay, I know not, nor can I conceive.

Bobadill. Why thus, sir. I would select nineteen more, to myself, throughout the land; gentlemen they should be of good spirit, strong and able constitution; I would choose them by an instinct, a character that I have: and I would teach these nineteen the special rules, as your punto, your reverso, your stoccata, your imbroccato, your passada, your montanto; till they could all play very near, or altogether as well as myself. This done, say the enemy were forty thousand strong, we twenty would come into the field the tenth of March, or thereabouts; and we would challenge twenty of the enemy; they could not in their honour refuse us: Well, we would kill them; challenge twenty more, kill them; twenty more, kill them; twenty more, kill them too; and thus would we kill every man his twenty a day, that's twenty score; twenty score, that's two hundred; two hundred a day, five days a thousand; forty thousand; forty times five, five times forty, two hundred days kills them all up by computation. And this will I venture my poor gentleman-like carcase to perform, provided there be no treason practised upon us, by fair and discreet manhood; that is, civilly by the sword.

E. Knowell. Why, are you so sure of your hand, captain, at all times?

Bobadill. Tut! never miss thrust, upon my reputation with you.

E. Knowell. I would not stand in Downright's state then, an you meet him, for the wealth of any one street in London.

Bobadill. Why, sir, you mistake me; if he were here now, by this welkin, I would not draw my weapon on him. Let this gentleman do his mind; but I will bastinado him, by the bright sun, wherever I meet him.

Matthew. Faith, and I'll have a fling at him, at my distance.

E. Knowell. Ods so, look where he is! yonder he goes.

DOWNRIGHT crosses the stage.

Downright. What peevish luck have I, I cannot meet with these bragging rascals?

Bobadill. It is not he, is it?

E. Knowell. Yes, faith, it is he.

Matthew. I'll be hanged then if that were he.

E. Knowell. Sir, keep your hanging good for some greater matter, for I assure you that were he.

Stephen. Upon my reputation, it was he.

Bobadill. Had I thought it had been he, he must not have gone so: but I can hardly be induced to think it was he yet.

E. Knowell. That I think, sir.

Re-enter DOWNRIGHT.

But see, he is come again.

Downright. O, Pharaoh's foot, have I found you? Come, draw to your tools; draw, gipsy, or I'll thrash you.

Bobadill. Gentleman of valour, I do believe in thee; hear me—

Downright. Draw your weapon then.

Bobadill. Tall man, I never thought on it till now— Body of me, I had a warrant of the peace served on me, even now as I came along, by a water-bearer; this gentleman saw it, Master Matthew.

Downright. 'Sdeath! you will not draw then?

Disarms and beats him. MATTHEW *runs away.*

Bobadill. Hold, hold! under thy favour forbear!

Downright. Prate again, as you like this, you— foist, you! You'll control the point, you! Your consort is gone; had he stay'd he had shared with you, sir.

Exit.

Bobadill. Well, gentlemen, bear witness, I was bound to the peace, by this good day.

E. Knowell. No, faith, it's an ill day, captain, never reckon it other: but, say you were bound to the peace, the law allows you to defend yourself: that will prove but a poor excuse.

Bobadill. I cannot tell, sir; I desire good construction in fair sort. I never sustain'd the like disgrace, by heaven! Sure I was struck by a planet thence, for I had no power to touch my weapon.

E. Knowell. Ay, like enough; I have heard of many that have been beaten under a planet: go, get you to a surgeon. 'Slid! an these be your tricks, your passadoes, and your montantos, I'll none of them.

Exit BOBADILL.

O, manners! that this age should bring forth such creatures! that nature should be at leisure to make them!

BEAUMONT AND FLETCHER

BEAUMONT.   BORN 1586.   DIED 1616.
FLETCHER.   BORN 1579.   DIED 1625.

BEAUMONT and FLETCHER are great names in the English Drama, but the demands commonly made by critics in their favour hardly seem to be justified if we are to apply to them the canons derived from the works of admitted masters of the stage. That Beaumont at least was a great poet his exquisite lyrics—hardly below Shakspere's own—abundantly testify. In romantic tragedy, too, the joint work of these great men was assuredly of the highest class, but I find little in their comedy-writings which is fit to stand on a level with their 'Philaster,' or their 'Maid's Tragedy.' Their comic method at its best was Jonson's method, but their work in this line will bear no sort of comparison with Jonson's. It is certain that half the prosperity of a good play, like that of a good jest, is in the audience. Though Beaumont and Fletcher wrote a few of their early plays before Shakspere's death, the bulk of them continued to be acted in the age after Shakspere's, when the times, and audiences with the times, had greatly changed: the earnest spirit of that great age had by then died out, or was confined to the Puritans. In reading the numerous comedies of Fletcher, the more practised and the more distinctly a comic dramatist of the two, it is impossible not to perceive that we are in the hands of one who is rather a clever playwright than a dramatist in the higher sense, of one who is no longer concerned as Marlowe, Shakspere, Peele, and Webster were concerned with the deeper and subtler springs of human emotion, but has his eye on a half-educated pit and gallery, which he knows are careless of the old music of the heroic line, who ask only for smart and easy dialogue in the fashion of the day, for bustle, for stage-trick, and for stage-movement. The reader of the comedies of Beaumont and Fletcher is for ever brought up by bits of coarse, rough, gross, or careless handiwork, far below the standard of the best work of the period. The popular taste of their day went further than ever before for extravagant metaphor, strained and affected phrases, and verbal puns and quibbles. Audiences got all this from our dramatists, but the result cannot pass as good comedy, the true canon for which has never been so clearly laid down as by Molière himself,

> 'Ce style figuré dont on fait vanité
> Sort du bon caractère et de la verité,
> Ce n'est que jeux de mots, qu'affectation pure
> Et ce n'est pas ainsi que peint la nature.'

BEAUMONT AND FLETCHER

A KING AND NO KING

CAPTAIN BESSUS is an adventurer and a rank coward, so much so that he is afraid even to run away by himself. 'I never was at battle but once, and there I was running, but Mardonius cudgelled me; yet I got loose at last, but was so afraid that I saw no more than my shoulders do, but fled with my whole company among my enemies and overthrew 'em.' So has he got a reputation for valour from having previously been esteemed a poltroon, and now those whom he had abused, 'call him freshly to account' thinking to 'get honour on him.'

A Room in the House of BESSUS.

Enter a Gentleman.

Gent. Good morrow, Captain Bessus.

Bessus. Good morrow, sir.

Gent. I come to speak with you—

Bes. You 're very welcome.

Gent. From one that holds himself wrong'd by you some three years since. Your worth he says is famed, and he doth nothing doubt but you will do him right, as beseems a soldier.

Bes. Aside. A plague on 'em! so they cry all.

Gent. And a slight note I have about me for you, for the delivery of which you must excuse me: it is an office that friendship calls upon me to do, and no way offensive to you; since I desire but right on both sides.

Gives a letter.

Bes. 'Tis a challenge, sir, is it not?

Gent. 'Tis an inviting to the field.

Bes. Aside. An inviting! Oh, cry you mercy! What a compliment he delivers it with! he might as agreeably to my nature present me poison with such a speech. (*Reads.*) Um — um — um — *Reputation* — um — um — um — *call you to account* — um — um — um — *forced to this* — um — um — um — *with my sword* — um — um — um — *like a gentleman* — um — um — um — *dear to me* — um — um — um — *satisfaction.* 'Tis very well, sir, I do accept it, but he must wait an answer this thirteen weeks.

Gent. Why, sir, he would be glad to wipe off this stain as quick as he could.

Bes. Sir, upon my credit, I am already engaged to two hundred and twelve; all which must have their stains wiped off, if that be the word, before him.

Gent. Sir, if you be truly engaged but to one, he shall stay a competent time.

Bes. Upon my faith, sir, to two hundred and twelve: And I have a spent body, too much bruised in battle;

so that I cannot fight, I must be plain, above three combats a day. All the kindness I can show him is to set him resolvedly in my roll the two hundred and thirteenth man, which is something; for, I tell you, I think there will be more after him than before him; I think so. Pray you commend me to him, and tell him this. *Exit Gentleman.*

Gent. I will, sir; good morrow to you.

Bes. Good morrow, good sir.—Certainly my safest way were to print myself a coward, with a discovery how I came by my credit, and clap it upon every post. I have received above thirty challenges within this two hours: Marry, all but the first I put off with engagement; and, by good fortune, the first is no madder of fighting than I; so that that's referred. The place where it must be ended is four day's journey off, and our arbitrators are these: he has chosen a gentleman in travel, and I have a special friend with a quartain ague, like to hold him this five years, for mine; and when his man comes home we are to expect my friend's health. If they would send me challenges thus thick, as long as I lived, I would have no other living; I can make seven shillings a day o' th' paper to the grocers. Yet I learn nothing by all these but a little skill in comparing of styles: I do find evidently that there is some one scrivener in this town, that has a great hand in writing of challenges, for they are all of a cut, and six of 'em in a hand; and they all end 'My reputation is dear to me and I must require satisfaction.'—Who's there? more paper, I hope. No, 'tis my lord Bacurius; I fear, all is not well betwixt us.

Enter BACURIUS.

Bac. Now, Captain Bessus! I come about a frivolous matter, caused by as idle a report: You know you were a coward.

Bes. Very right.

Bac. And wrong'd me.

Bes. True, my lord.

Bac. But now, people will call you valiant; desertlessly, I think; yet, for their satisfaction, I will have you fight with me.

Bes. Oh, my good lord, my deep engagements—

Bac. Tell me not of your engagements, Captain Bessus! It is not to be put off with an excuse. For my own part, I am none of the multitude that believe your conversion from coward.

Bes. My lord, I seek not quarrels, and this belongs not to me; I am not to maintain it.

Bac. Who then pray?

Bes. Bessus the coward wrong'd you.

Bac. Right.

Bes. And shall Bessus the valiant maintain what Bessus the coward did?

Bac. I pr'ythee leave these cheating tricks! I swear

thou shalt fight with me, or thou shalt be beaten extremely, and kick'd.

Bes. Since you provoke me thus far, my lord, I will fight with you; and, by my sword, it shall cost me twenty pounds, but I will have my leg well a week sooner purposely.

Bac. Your leg! why, what ails your leg? I'll do a cure on you. Stand up! *Kicks him.*

Bes. My lord, this is not noble in you.

Bac. What dost thou with such a phrase in thy mouth? I will kick thee out of all good words before I leave thee. *Kicks him.*

Bes. My lord, I take this as a punishment for the offence I did when I was a coward.

Bac. When thou wert? Confess thyself a coward still, or, by this light, I'll beat thee into sponge.

Bes. Why, I am one.

Bac. Are you so, sir? and why do you wear a sword, then? Come, unbuckle! quick!

Bes. My lord?

Bac. Unbuckle, I say, and give it me; or, as I live, thy head will ache extremely.

Bes. It is a pretty hilt; and if your lordship take an affection to it, with all my heart I present it to you for a new-year's-gift.

  Gives his sword, with a knife in the scabbard.

Bac. I thank you very heartily, sweet captain! Farewell.

Bes. One word more : I beseech your lordship to render me my knife again.

Bac. Marry, by all means, captain.
Gives him back the knife.
Cherish yourself with it, and eat hard, good captain : we cannot tell whether we have any more such. Adieu, dear captain. *Exit.*

WYCHERLEY

BORN 1640. DIED 1715.

WYCHERLEY has this merit, that he was first in the field of our best school of comedy-writers. He virtually began the school of the Restoration comic dramatists, the so-called comedy of manners. True it is that had Molière not written comedies Wycherley would not have written as he did, and it must be admitted that Sir George Etheredge wrote plays as unconventionally natural so far as dialogue is concerned as Wycherley's; but Etheredge's comedies are altogether beneath notice as literature, while Wycherley is, and ever will be, a true English classic. If he transferred to our stage whole scenes from Molière, he did them into strong, nervous English, racy with mother wit. Wycherley was a man of the world who lived in and knew intimately the little world of Charles II.'s day. The talk of courtiers and court ladies was the talk that was most familiar to him; their sentiments were his, their grossness was his, and their morality was not repugnant to him. He brought their talk, sentiments, grossness, and morals before the footlights. Few men—even the ablest—can bear in mind, when they write for the stage, that the dramatic art is a thing apart from and beside the literary art; that the time-followed devices and artifices of men of letters are thrown away on actors and audiences—in short, that plays are not books. Wycherley was but following the example of a far greater master of the art than himself—of Molière—when he transferred the language of daily life to the stage—adding the point and trenchant vigour which it seldom possesses in daily life. That he did all this, and struck the first note of what now passes in the world as true comedy, is Wycherley's claim to immortality. If we read his 'Plain Dealer' or his 'Country Wife' after reading the 'Merry Wives of Windsor,' the nearest to modern comedy of all Shakspere's plays, we shall appreciate Wycherley's service to the English drama.

WYCHERLEY

THE PLAIN DEALER

THE scene passes between Olivia, Eliza (her cousin), Lettice (her maid), and Mr. Novel and Lord Plausible, her friends and visitors.

Olivia has won the affections of Manly, the Plain Dealer, a hater of falseness and frivolity, by her affectation of great down-rightness, sincerity, and strictness of conduct. She rails in public at the fashions and follies of the world, which she secretly loves and practises. She deceives Manly, privately marries his bosom friend, and attempts to steal his money, left in her care. Eventually Manly's eyes are opened, and Olivia's conduct is publicly exposed.

OLIVIA'S Lodgings.

Enter OLIVIA, ELIZA, and LETTICE.

Olivia. Ah, cousin, what a world 'tis we live in ! I am so weary of it.

Eliza. Truly, cousin, I can find no fault with it, but that we cannot always live in 't, for I can never be weary of it.

Olivia. Oh hideous ! You cannot be in earnest, sure, when you say you like the filthy world.

Eliza. You cannot be in earnest, sure, when you say you dislike it.

Olivia. You are a very censorious creature, I find.

Eliza. I must confess I think we women as often discover where we love by our railing, as men when they lie by their swearing. . . . But is it possible the world, which has such variety of charms for other women, can have none for you? Let's see—first, what d' ye think of dressing and fine clothes?

Olivia. Dressing! Fy, fy, 'tis my aversion. (*To* LETTICE.) But come hither, you dowdy; methinks you might have opened this toure better; O hideous! I cannot suffer it! D' ye see how 't sits?

Eliza. Well enough, cousin, if dressing be your aversion.

Olivia. 'Tis so; and for variety of rich clothes, they are more my aversion.

Lettice. Ay, 'tis because your ladyship wears 'em too long; for indeed a gown, like a gallant, grows one's aversion by having too much of it.

Olivia. Insatiable creature! I'll be sworn I have had this not above three days, cousin, and within this month have made some six more.

Eliza. Then your aversion to 'em is not altogether so great.

Olivia. Alas! 'tis for my woman only I wear 'em, cousin.

Lettice. If it be for me only, madam, pray do not wear 'em.

Eliza. But what d'ye think of visits—balls?

Olivia. O, I detest 'em.

Eliza. Of plays?

Olivia. I abominate 'em; filthy, hideous things.

Eliza. What say you to masquerading in the winter, and Hyde-park in the summer?

Olivia. Insipid pleasures I taste not.

Eliza. Indeed! But let's see—will nothing please you? what d' ye think of the court?

Olivia. How, the court! the court, cousin! my aversion, my aversion, my aversion of all aversions!

Eliza. How, the court! where—

Olivia. Where sincerity is a quality as much out of fashion and as unprosperous as bashfulness: I could not laugh at a quibble, though it were a fat privy-counsellor's; nor praise a lord's ill verses, though I were myself the subject; nor an old lady's young looks, though I were her woman; nor sit to a vain young smile-maker, though he flattered me. In short, I could not glout upon a man when he comes into a room, and laugh at him when he goes out: I cannot rail at the absent to flatter the standers-by; I—

Eliza. Well, but railing now is so common, that 'tis no more malice, but the fashion; and the absent think they are no more the worse for being railed at, than the present think they're the better for being flattered. And for the court—

Olivia. Nay, do not defend the court; for you'll make me rail at it like a trusting citizen's widow.

Eliza. Or like a Holborn lady, who could not get in to the last ball, or was out of countenance in the drawing-room the last Sunday of her appearance there. For none rail at the court but those who cannot get into it, or else who are ridiculous when they are there ; and I shall suspect you were laughed at when you were last there, or would be a maid of honour.

Olivia. I a maid of honour! To be a maid of honour, were of all things yet my aversion.

Eliza. In what sense am I to understand you? But in fine, by the word aversion, I'm sure you dissemble; for I never knew woman yet used it who did not. Come, our tongues belie our hearts more than our pocket-glasses do our faces. But methinks we ought to leave off dissembling, since 'tis grown of no use to us; for all wise observers understand us now-a-days, as they do dreams, almanacs, and Dutch gazettes, by the contrary : and a man no more believes a woman when she says she has an aversion for him, than when—

Olivia. O hideous! Peace, cousin, or your discourse will be my aversion : and you may believe me.

Eliza. Yes ; for if anything be a woman's aversion, 'tis plain dealing from another woman : and perhaps that's your quarrel to the world; for that will talk.

Olivia. Talk? not of me sure; for what men do I converse with? what visits do I admit?

Enter Boy.

Boy. Here's the gentleman to wait upon you, madam.

Olivia. On me! you little unthinking fop; d'ye know what you say?

Boy. Yes, madam, 'tis the gentleman that comes every day to you, who—

Olivia. Hold your peace, you heedless little animal, and get you gone.— *Exit Boy.*
This country boy, cousin, takes my dancing-master, tailor, or the spruce milliner, for visitors.

Lettice. No, madam; 'tis Mr. Novel, I'm sure, by his talking so loud: I know his voice too, madam.

Olivia. You know nothing, you buffle-headed stupid creature you: you would make my cousin believe I receive visits. But if it be Mr.——what did you call him?

Lettice. Mr. Novel, madam; he that—

Olivia. Hold your peace; I'll hear no more of him. But if it be your Mr.——(I cannot think of his name again) I suppose he has followed my cousin hither.

Eliza. No, cousin, I will not rob you of the honour of the visit: 'tis to you, cousin; for I know him not.

Olivia. Nor did I ever hear of him before, upon my honour, cousin; besides, han't I told you, that visits, and the business of visits, flattery and detraction, are my aversion? D'ye think then I would admit such a coxcomb as he is? who rather than not rail will rail at the dead, whom none speak ill of; rather than not flatter, will flatter the poets of the age, whom none will flatter; who affects novelty as much as the fashion, and is as fantastical as changeable, and as well known as the fashion; who likes nothing but what is new, nay, would choose to have his friend or his title a new one. In fine, he is my aversion.

Eliza. I find you do know him, cousin; at least, have heard of him.

Olivia. Yes, now I remember, I have heard of him.

Eliza. Well; but since he is such a coxcomb, for heaven's sake, let him not come up. Tell him, Mrs. Lettice, your lady is not within.

Olivia. No, Lettice, tell him my cousin is here, and that he may come up. For notwithstanding I detest the sight of him, you may like his conversation; and though I would use him scurvily, I will not be rude to you in my own lodging: since he has followed you hither, let him come up, I say.

Eliza. Very fine! pray let him go to the devil, I say, for me: I know him not, nor desire it. Send him away, Mrs. Lettice.

Olivia. Upon my word, she shan't: I must disobey your commands, to comply with your desires. Call him up, Lettice.

Eliza. Nay, I'll swear she shall not stir on that errand. *Holds* LETTICE.

Olivia. Well then, I'll call him myself for you, since you will have it so. *Calls out at the door.* Mr. Novel, sir, sir!

Enter NOVEL.

Novel. Madam, I beg your pardon; perhaps you were busy: I did not think you had company with you.

Eliza. Aside to OLIVIA. Yet he comes to me, cousin!

Olivia. Chairs there. *They sit.*

Novel. Well; but, madam, d'ye know whence I come now?

Olivia. From some melancholy place, I warrant, sir, since they have lost your good company.

Eliza. So!

Novel. From a place where they have treated me at dinner with so much civility and kindness, a plague on them! that I could hardly get away to you, dear madam.

Olivia. You have a way with you so new and obliging, sir!

Eliza. Apart to OLIVIA. You hate flattery, cousin!

Novel. Nay, faith, madam, d'ye think my way new? Then you are obliging, madam. I must confess, I hate imitation, to do anything like other people. All that know me do me the honour to say, I am an original, faith. But, as I was saying, madam, I have been treated to-day with all the ceremony and kindness imaginable at my Lady Autumn's. But, the nauseous old woman at the upper end of her table—

Olivia. Revives the old Grecian custom, of serving in a death's head with their banquets.

Novel. Ha! ha! fine, just, i' faith, nay, and new. 'Tis like eating with the ghost in the '*Libertine*': she would frighten a man from her dinner with her hollow invitation—

Olivia. I detest her hollow cherry cheeks: she looks like an old coach new painted; affecting an unseemly smugness, whilst she is ready to drop in pieces.

Eliza. Apart to OLIVIA. You hate detraction, I see, cousin.

Novel. But the silly old fury, whilst she affects to look like a woman of this age, talks—

Olivia. Like one of the last; and as passionately as an old courtier who has outlived his office.

Novel. Yes, madam; but pray let me give you her character. Then she never counts her age by the years, but—

Olivia. By the masques she has lived to see.

Novel. Nay then, madam, I see you think a little harmless railing too great a pleasure for any but yourself; and therefore I've done.

Olivia. Nay, faith, you shall tell me who you had there at dinner.

Novel. If you would hear me, madam.

Olivia. Most patiently; speak, sir.

Novel. Then, we had her daughter—

Olivia. Ay, her daughter; the very disgrace to good clothes, which she always wears but to heighten her deformity, not mend it: for she is still most splendidly, gallantly ugly, and looks like an ill piece of daubing in a rich frame.

Novel. So! But have you done with her, madam? and can you spare her to me a little now?

Olivia. Ay, ay, sir.

Novel. Then, she is like—

Olivia. She is, you'd say, like a city bride; the greater fortune, but not the greater beauty, for her dress.

Novel. Well: yet have you done, madam? Then she—

Olivia. Then she bestows as unfortunately upon her face all the graces in fashion, as the languishing eye, the hanging or pouting lip. . . . But, Mr. Novel, who had you besides at dinner?

Novel. Nay, the devil take me if I tell you, unless you will allow me the privilege of railing in my turn. —But, now I think on 't, the women ought to be your province, as the men are mine: and you must know we had him whom—

Olivia. Him whom—

Novel. What, invading me already? and giving the character before you know the man?

Eliza. No, that is not fair, though it be usual.

Novel. Then, I say, we had that familiar coxcomb, who is at home wheresoe'er he comes.

Olivia. Ay, that fool—

Novel. Nay then, madam, your servant; I'm gone. Taking the fool out of one's mouth is worse than taking the bread out of one's mouth.

Olivia. I've done; your pardon, Mr. Novel: pray proceed.

Novel. I say, the rogue, that he may be the only wit in company, will let nobody else talk, and—

Olivia. Ay, those fops who love to talk all themselves are of all things my aversion.

Novel. Then you'll let me speak, madam, sure. The rogue, I say, will force his jest upon you; and I hate a jest that's forced upon a man, as much as a glass.

Eliza. Why, I hope, sir, he does not expect a man of your temperance in jesting should do him reason?

Novel. What! interruption from this side too? I must then— *Offers to rise,* OLIVIA *holds him.*

Olivia. No, sir.—But who else, prithee Mr. Novel, was there with you? Nay, thou shan't stir.

Novel. I beg your pardon, madam; I cannot stay in any place where I'm not allowed a little Christian liberty of railing.

Olivia. Nay, prithee Mr. Novel, stay: and though you should rail at me, I would hear you with patience. Prithee who else was there with you?

Novel. Your servant, madam.

Olivia. Nay, prithee tell us, Mr. Novel, prithee do.

Novel. We had nobody else.

Olivia. Nay, faith, I know you had. Come, my Lord Plausible was there too; who is, cousin, a—

Eliza. You need not tell me what he is, cousin; for I know him to be a civil, good-natured, harmless gentleman, that speaks well of all the world, and is always in good humour; and—

Olivia. Hold, cousin, hold; I hate detraction. But I must tell you, cousin, his civility is cowardice, his good-nature want of wit, and he has neither courage nor sense to rail: and for his being always in humour, 'tis because he is never dissatisfied with himself. In fine, he is my aversion; and I never admit his visits beyond my hall.

Novel. No, he visit you! Damn him, cringing grinning rogue! if I should see him coming up to you, I would make bold to kick him down again.—Ha!

Enter Lord PLAUSIBLE.

My dear lord, your most humble servant.

Rises and salutes PLAUSIBLE and kisses him.

Eliza. Aside. So, I find kissing and railing succeed each other with the angry men as well as with the angry women; and their quarrels are like love quarrels, since absence is the only cause of them; for as soon as the man appears again, they are over.

Lord Plausible. Your most faithful humble servant, generous Mr. Novel. And, madam, I am your eternal slave, and kiss your fair hands; which I had done sooner, according to your commands, but—

Olivia. No excuses, my lord.

Eliza. Apart to OLIVIA. What, you sent for him then, cousin?

Novel. Aside. Ha! invited!

Olivia. I know you must divide yourself; for your good company is too general a good to be engrossed by any particular friend.

Lord Plausible. O lord, madam, my company! your most obliged, faithful, humble servant. But I could have brought you good company indeed; for I parted at your door with two of the worthiest, bravest men.

Olivia. Who were they, my lord?

Novel. Who do you call the worthiest, bravest men, pray?

Lord Plausible. O, the wisest, bravest gentlemen! men of such honour and virtue! of such good qualities! ah!—

Eliza. Aside. This is a coxcomb that speaks ill of all people a different way, and libels everybody with dull praise, and commonly in the wrong place; so makes his panegyrics abusive lampoons.

Olivia. But pray let me know who they were?

Lord Plausible. Ah! such patterns of heroic virtue! such—

Novel. Well; but who the devil are they?

Lord Plausible. The honour of our nation! the glory of our age! Ah, I could dwell a twelvemonth on their praise; which indeed I might spare by telling their names; Sir John Current and Sir Richard Court-Title.

Novel. Court-Title! ha! ha!

Olivia. And sir John Current! Why will you keep such a wretch company, my lord?

Lord Plausible. O madam, seriously you are a little too severe; for he is a man of unquestioned reputation in everything.

Olivia. Yes, because he endeavours only with the women to pass for a man of courage, and with the bullies for a wit; with the wits for a man of business, and with the men of business for a favourite at court; and at court for city-security.

Novel. And for sir Richard, he—

Lord Plausible. He loves your choice picked company, persons that—

Olivia. He loves a lord indeed; but—

Novel. Pray, dear madam, let me have but a bold stroke or two at his picture. He loves a lord, as you say, though—

Olivia. Though he borrowed his money, and ne'er paid him again.

Novel. And would bespeak a place three days before at the back-end of a lord's coach to Hyde-park.

Lord Plausible. Nay, i' faith, i' faith, you are both too severe.

Olivia. Then to show yet more his passion for quality, he makes love to that fulsome coach-load of honour, my Lady Goodly, for he's always at her lodging.

Lord Plausible. Because it is the conventicle-gallant, the meeting-house of all the fair ladies, and glorious superfine beauties of the town.

Novel. Very fine ladies! there's first—

Olivia. Her honour, as fat as an hostess.

Lord Plausible. She is something plump indeed, a goodly, comely, graceful person.

Novel. Then there's my lady Frances—what d'ye call her? as ugly—

Lord Plausible. She has wit in abundance, and the handsomest heel, elbow, and tip of an ear, you ever saw.

Novel. Heel and elbow! ha! ha! And there's my lady Betty, you know—

Olivia. As sluttish and slatternly as an Irishwoman bred in France.

Lord Plausible. Ah! all she has hangs with a loose air, indeed, and becoming negligence.

Eliza. You see all faults with lovers' eyes, I find, my lord.

Lord Plausible. Ah, madam, your most obliged, faithful, humble servant to command! But you can say nothing sure of the superfine mistress—

Olivia. I know who you mean. She is as censorious and detracting a jade as a superannuated sinner.

Lord Plausible. She has a smart way of raillery, 'tis confessed.

Novel. And there for Mrs. Grideline—

Lord Plausible. She, I'm sure, is—

Olivia. One that never spoke ill of anybody, 'tis confessed. For she is as silent in conversation as a country lover, and no better company than a clock or a weather-glass; for if she sounds, 'tis but once an hour to put you in mind of the time of day, or to tell you 'twill be cold or hot, rain or snow.

Lord Plausible. Ah, poor creature! she's extremely good and modest.

Novel. And for Mrs. Bridlechin, she's—

Olivia. As proud as a churchman's wife.

Lord Plausible. She's a woman of great spirit and honour, and will not make herself cheap, 'tis true.

Novel. Then Mrs. Hoyden, that calls all people by their surnames, and is—

Olivia. As familiar a duck—

Novel. As an actress in the tiring-room. There I was once beforehand with you, madam.

Lord Plausible. Mrs. Hoyden! a poor, affable, good-natured soul. But the divine Mrs. Trifle comes thither too. Sure her beauty, virtue, and conduct, you can say nothing to.

G

Olivia. No!

Novel. No!—Pray let me speak, madam.

Olivia. First, can any one be called beautiful that squints?

Lord Plausible. Her eyes languish a little, I own.

Novel. Languish! ha! ha!

Olivia. Languish!—Then, for her conduct, she was seen at the 'Country Wife' after the first day. There's for you, my lord.

VANBRUGH

Born 1666.   Died 1726.

Of the four great Restoration playwrights, VANBRUGH had most of the 'trick of the stage.' Like Wycherley, he has the rare and great merit that he wrote to be acted, not to be read. He is less cynical than Wycherley, more civilized and human in his satire, and far less gross. He lacks the wit and style of Congreve, but has greater natural flow and natural ease: the players are said to have found his pieces particularly easy to get by heart, and this would seem to be a proof that he spoke the language natural to his day. Vanbrugh goes further afield for his plots than his contemporaries, and brings more than mere fine ladies and gentlemen on to the stage. The acting quality of his plays is often admirable, and by no means lost even in the reading. He must be a dull reader, for instance, who does not see the good broad fun and the opportunity for telling by-play in the hands of a capable actress, in the scene where the fond and foolish mother of Dick Amlet interrupts his talk with interjections of her personal admiration for her scapegrace son—'*What a nose he has!*'—'*What a cherry cheek is there!*'—'*Now, the Lord love thee, for thou art a comfortable young man!*' The part of Lord Foppington in 'The Relapse' was as famous in its day as Lord Dundreary in ours. If there is a blemish in the character it is one that could ill be spared: it is that Lord Foppington is far too witty: in real life a man so capable of poignant, shrewd, and ready speech would not have laid his own folly and heartlessness so bare. Lord Foppington is not quite original; the foundations of the character were laid by Etheredge in his 'Sir Fopling Flutter,' though Sir Fopling is but a feeble fool and a monotonous one, in comparison with his lordship, 'a poor, thin curd of ass's milk': half the fun of him is in his name, and he is wholly incapable of that famous exordium which Lord Foppington makes when, having by the intrigue of the play got into a humiliating scrape, lost Miss Hoyden and her great fortune, and been baffled in all his self-seeking schemes, he preserves his imperturbability to the last, and winds up with that speech which is half impertinence, half philosophy, and wholly wit: '*Dear Tam, since things are thus fallen aut, prithee give me leave to wish thee jay de bon cœur, strike me dumb; you have married a woman beautiful in her person, charming in her airs, prudent in her conduct, constant in her inclinations, and of a nice marality, split my windpipe!*'

VANBRUGH

A JOURNEY TO LONDON

LORD LOVERULE, whose tastes incline to home comforts and a quiet, domestic life, has been reproving his wife, Lady Arabella, for her love of fashionable society, late hours, and dissipation. She relates their dispute to Clarinda, her cousin, who describes the life she would herself choose to lead, with a moderate and judicious use of social pleasures.

A Room in Lord LOVERULE'S *House.*

Lady ARABELLA. *Enter* CLARINDA.

Clarinda. Good morrow, madam; how do you do to-day? You seem to be in a little fluster.

Lady Arabella. My lord has been in one, and as I am the most complaisant poor creature in the world, I put myself into one too, purely to be suitable company to him.

Clarinda. You are prodigious good; but surely it must be mighty agreeable when a man and his wife can give themselves the same turn of conversation.

Lady Arabella. Oh, the prettiest thing in the world!

Clarinda. But yet, though I believe there's no life

so happy as a married one, in the main; yet I fancy, where two people are so very much together, they must often be in want of something to talk upon.

Lady Arabella. Clarinda, you are the most mistaken in the world; married people have things to talk of, child, that never enter into the imagination of others. Why now, here's my lord and I, we han't been married above two short years, you know, and we have already eight or ten things constantly in bank, that whenever we want company, we can talk of any one of them for two hours together, and the subject never the flatter. It will be as fresh next day, if we have occasion for it, as it was the first day it entertained us.

Clarinda. Why, that must be wonderful pretty.

Lady Arabella. Oh, there's no life like it! This very day now, for example, my lord and I, after a pretty cheerful *tête-à-tête* dinner, sat down by the fireside, in an idle, indolent, picktooth way for a while, as if we had not thought of one another's being in the room. At last (stretching himself and yawning twice), My dear, says he, you came home very late last night. 'Twas but two in the morning, says I. I was in bed (yawning) by eleven, says he. So you are every night, says I. Well, says he, I am amazed how you can sit up so late. How can you be amazed, says I, at a thing which happens so often? Upon which we entered into conversation. And though this is a point has entertained us above fifty times already, we always find so many pretty new things to say upon 't, that I believe in my soul it will last as long as we live.

Clarinda. But in such sort of family dialogues (though extremely well for passing of time) don't there now and then enter some little witty sort of bitterness?

Lady Arabella. Oh yes; which don't do amiss at all, a little something that's sharp, moderates the extreme sweetness of matrimonial society, which would else perhaps be cloying. Though, to tell you the truth, Clarinda, I think we squeezed a little too much lemon into it this bout; for it grew so sour at last, that I think I almost told him he was a fool; and he talked something oddly of turning me out of doors.

Clarinda. Oh, but have a care of that!

Lady Arabella. Why, to be serious, Clarinda, what would you have a woman do in my case? There is no one thing he can do in this world to please me—except giving me money; and that he is growing weary of; and I at the same time (partly by nature, and partly perhaps by keeping the best company) do with my soul love almost everything that he hates. I dote upon assemblies, adore masquerades, my heart bounds at a ball; I love play to distraction, cards enchant me, and dice—put me out of my little wits.—Dear, dear hazard, what music there is in the rattle of the dice, compared to a sleepy opera! Do you ever play at hazard, Clarinda?

Clarinda. Never; I don't think it sits well upon women; it's very masculine, and has too much of a rake; you see how it makes the men swear and curse. Sure it must incline the women to do the same too, if they durst give way to it.

Lady Arabella. So it does; but hitherto, for a little decency, we keep it in; and when, in spite of our teeth, an oath gets into our mouths, we swallow it.

Clarinda. That's enough to burst you; but in time perhaps you'll let 'em fly as they do.

Lady Arabella. Why, 'tis probable we may, for the pleasure of all polite women's lives now, you know, is founded upon entire liberty to do what they will. But shall I tell you what happened t' other night? Having lost all my money but ten melancholy guineas, and throwing out for them, what do you think slipped from me?

Clarinda. An oath?

Lady Arabella. Gud soons!

Clarinda. O Lord! O Lord! Did not it frighten you out of your wits?

Lady Arabella. Clarinda, I thought a gun had gone off.—But I forget, you are a prude, and design to live soberly.

Clarinda. Why, 'tis true; both my nature and education do a good deal incline me that way.

Lady Arabella. Well, surely to be sober is to be terribly dull. You will marry, won't you?

Clarinda. I can't tell but I may.

Lady Arabella. And you'll live in town?

Clarinda. Half the year I should like it very well.

Lady Arabella. And you would live in London half a year, to be sober in it?

Clarinda. Yes.

Lady Arabella. Why can't you as well go and be sober in the country?

Clarinda. So I would the t' other half year.

Lady Arabella. And pray what pretty scheme of life would you form now, for your summer and winter sober entertainments?

Clarinda. A scheme that, I think, might very well content us.

Lady Arabella. Let's hear it.

Clarinda. I could in summer pass my time very agreeably, in riding soberly, in walking soberly, in sitting under a tree soberly, in gardening soberly, in reading soberly, in hearing a little music soberly, in conversing with some agreeable friends soberly, in working soberly, in managing my family and children (if I had any) soberly, and possibly by these means I might induce my husband to be as sober as myself.

Lady Arabella. Well, Clarinda, thou art a most contemptible creature. But let's have the sober town scheme too, for I'm charmed with the country one.

Clarinda. You shall, and I'll try to stick to my sobriety there too.

Lady Arabella. If you do, you'll make me sick of you. But let's hear it, however.

Clarinda. I would entertain myself in observing the new fashions soberly, I would please myself in new clothes soberly, I would divert myself with agreeable friends at home and abroad soberly, I would play at quadrille soberly, I would go to court soberly, I would go to some plays soberly, I would go to operas soberly, and I think I could go once, or, if I liked my company, twice to a masquerade soberly.

Lady Arabella. If it had not been for that last piece of sobriety, I was going to call for some surfeit-water.

Clarinda. Why don't you think, that with the further aid of breakfasting, dining, supping, and sleeping (not to say a word of devotion), the four-and-twenty hours might roll over in a tolerable manner?

Lady Arabella. How I detest that word, tolerable!

THE RELAPSE: OR VIRTUE IN DANGER

MR. LOVELESS and Amanda, a young married couple, have come to town after spending their honeymoon in the country, and are visited by Berinthia, a young widow, Amanda's cousin, and Lord Foppington, formerly Sir Novelty Fashion, an empty-headed coxcomb who has just bought his title, and goes the rounds of his acquaintance to be congratulated upon it. He describes to the ladies the daily occupations of a man of fashion.

A Room in LOVELESS'S *Town-house.*
LOVELESS, AMANDA, BERINTHIA. *Enter Lord* FOPPINGTON.

Lord Foppington. Sir, I am your most humble servant.

Loveless. I wish you joy, my lord.

Lord Foppington. O Lard, sir !—Madam, your ladyship's welcome to tawn.

Amanda. I wish your lordship joy.

Lord Foppington. O Heavens, madam—

Loveless. My lord, this young lady is a relation of my wife's.

Lord Foppington. Saluting BERINTHIA. The beautifullest race of people upon earth, rat me! Dear Loveless, I am overjoyed to see you have brought your family to tawn again; I am, stap my vitals! *To* AMANDA. Far Gad's sake, madam, haw has your ladyship been able to subsist thus long, under the fatigue of a country life?

Amanda. My life has been very far from that, my lord; it has been a very quiet one.

Lord Foppington. Why, that's the fatigue I speak of, madam. For 'tis impossible to be quiet without thinking; now thinking is to me the greatest fatigue in the world.

Amanda. Does not your lordship love reading then?

Lord Foppington. Oh, passionately, madam.—But I never think of what I read.

Berinthia. But can your lordship read without thinking?

Lord Foppington. O Lard!—can your ladyship pray without devotion, madam?

Amanda. Well, I must own I think books the best entertainment in the world.

Lord Foppington. I am so much of your ladyship's mind, madam, that I have a private gallery, where I walk sometimes, is furnished with nothing but books and looking-glasses. Madam, I have gilded 'em and ranged 'em so prettily, before Gad, it is the most entertaining thing in the world to walk and look upon 'em.

Amanda. Nay, I love a neat library too; but 'tis, I think, the inside of a book should recommend it most to us.

Lord Foppington. That, I must confess, I am not altogether so fand of. Far to mind the inside of a book, is to entertain one's self with the forced product of another man's brain. Naw I think a man of quality and breeding may be much better diverted with the natural sprauts of his own. But to say the truth, madam, let a man love reading never so well, when once he comes to know this tawn, he finds so many better ways of passing away the four-and-twenty hours, that 'twere ten thousand pities he should consume his time in that. Far example, madam, my life; my life, madam, is a perpetual stream of pleasure, that glides through such a variety of entertainments, I believe the wisest of our ancestors never had the least conception of any of 'em. I rise, madam, about ten a-clack. I don't rise sooner because 'tis the worst thing in the world for the complexion; nat that I pretend to be a beau; but a man must endeavour to look wholesome, lest he make so nauseous a figure in the side-bax, the ladies should be compelled to turn their eyes upon the play. So at ten a-clack, I say, I rise. Naw, if I find it a good day, I resalve to take a turn in the Park, and see the fine women; so huddle on my clothes, and get dressed by one. If it be nasty weather, I take a turn in the chocolate-hause : where as you walk, madam, you have the prettiest prospect in the world; you have looking-glasses all round you.—But I'm afraid I tire the company.

Berinthia. Not at all. Pray go on.

Lord Foppington. Why then, ladies, from thence I go to dinner at Lacket's, where you are so nicely and delicately served, that, stap my vitals ! they shall compose you a dish no bigger than a saucer, shall come to fifty shillings. Between eating my dinner (and washing my mouth, ladies) I spend my time till I go to the play; where, till nine a-clack, I entertain myself with looking upon the company; and usually dispose of one hour more in leading them aut. So there's twelve of the four-and-twenty pretty well over. The other twelve, madam, are disposed of in two articles : in the first four I toast myself drunk, and in t' other eight I sleep myself sober again. Thus, ladies, you see my life is an eternal raund O of delights.

Loveless. 'Tis a heavenly one, indeed. . . . But your lordship is now become a pillar of the state; you must attend the weighty affairs of the nation.

Lord Foppington. Sir,—as to weighty affairs—I leave them to weighty heads. I never intend mine shall be a burden to my body.

Loveless. O but you'll find the house will expect your attendance.

Lord Foppington. Sir, you'll find the house will compound for my appearance.

Loveless. But your friends will take it ill if you don't attend their particular causes.

Lord Foppington. Not, sir, if I come time enough to give 'em my particular vote.

Berinthia. But pray, my lord, how do you dispose of yourself on Sundays? for that, methinks, should hang wretchedly on your hands.

Lord Foppington. Why faith, madam—Sunday—is a vile day, I must confess. I intend to move for leave to bring in a bill, that players may work upon it, as well as the hackney-coaches. Though this I must say for the government, it leaves us the churches to entertain us.—But then again, they begin so abominably early, a man must rise by candle-light to get dressed by the psalm.

Berinthia. Pray which church does your lordship most oblige with your presence?

Lord Foppington. Oh! St. James's, madam: there's much the best company.

Amanda. Is there good preaching too?

Lord Foppington. Why faith, madam—I can't tell. A man must have very little to do there that can give an account of the sermon.

Berinthia. You can give us an account of the ladies at least.

Lord Foppington. Or I deserve to be excommunicated.—There is my lady Tattle, my lady Prate, my lady Titter, my lady Leer, my lady Giggle, and my lady Grin. These sit in the front of the boxes, and all church-time are the prettiest company in the world stap my vitals! *To AMANDA.* Mayn't we hope for the honour to see your ladyship added to our society, madam?

Amanda. Alas, my lord! I am the worst company in the world at church: I'm apt to mind the prayers, or the sermon, or—

Lord Foppington. One is indeed strangely apt at church to mind what one should not do. But I hope, madam, at one time or other, I shall have the honour to lead your ladyship to your coach there.

THE CONFEDERACY

Dick Amlet is the son of old Mrs. Amlet, a seller of all sorts of 'toilet affairs' to ladies. He is a gamester and adventurer, but passes himself off as Colonel Shapely, a man of fortune. Brass, his friend and confederate, passes for his valet. Dick Amlet, with the aid of Flippanta, her maid, designs to marry Corinna, the daughter of Gripe, a rich money-scrivener, and possessing a fortune in her own right. He imposes for a time upon Clarissa, Gripe's second wife, and her friend Araminta, but is at last exposed by Mrs. Amlet, angry at his denial of their relationship.

Corinna is silent while the others all revile him, upon which Mrs. Amlet relents, and boasts of the large fortune she can give him; and Corinna declares she will still marry him.

The Street before Gripe's *House.*

Enter Brass.

Brass. Well, surely through the world's wide extent, there never appeared so impudent a fellow as my schoolfellow Dick.—Pass himself upon the town for a gentleman, drop into all the best company with an easy air, as if his natural element were in the sphere of quality; when the rogue had a kettledrum to his father, who was hanged for robbing a church, and has a pedlar to his mother—who carries her shop under her arm!—

. . . . . , . . .

A Room in Mrs. AMLET'S *House.*

Enter DICK AMLET.

Dick. Where's this old woman?—A-hey! What the devil, nobody at home! Ha! her strong box! and the key in't! 'tis so. Now Fortune be my friend. What the deuse!—not a penny of money in cash!—nor a chequer note!—nor a bank bill!—

Searches the strong box.

Nor a crooked stick! nor a—mum!—here's something.—A diamond necklace, by all the gods! Oons, the old woman!—Zest!

Enter Mrs. AMLET. DICK *claps the necklace in his pocket, then runs and asks her blessing.*

Pray, mother—

Mrs. Amlet. Is it possible!—Dick upon his humble knee! Ah my dear child!—May Heaven be good unto thee.

Dick. I'm come, my dear mother, to pay my duty to you, and to ask your consent to—

Mrs. Amlet. What a shape is there!

Dick. To ask your consent, I say, to marry a great fortune; for what is riches in this world without a blessing? and how can there be a blessing without respect and duty to parents?

Mrs. Amlet. What a nose he has!

Dick. And therefore, it being the duty of every good

child not to dispose of himself in marriage, without the—

Mrs. Amlet. Now the Lord love thee!—*Kissing him.* for thou art a goodly young man. Well, Dick,—and how goes it with the lady? Are her eyes open to thy charms? does she see what's for her own good? ha! is all sure? Hast thou broke a piece of money with her? Speak, bird, do: don't be modest and hide thy love from thy mother, for I 'm an indulgent parent.

Dick. Nothing under heaven can prevent my good fortune but its being discovered I am your son—

Mrs. Amlet. Then thou art still ashamed of thy natural mother—graceless! why, my reputation's as good as the best of them, you rascal you!

Dick. Lord, that is not the thing we talk of, mother; but—

Mrs. Amlet. I think, as the world goes, they may be proud of marrying their daughter into a vartuous family.

Dick. Oons! Vartue is not the case—

Mrs. Amlet. Where she may have a good example before her eyes.

Dick. I tell you, 'sdeath, I tell you—

Mrs. Amlet. Don't you swear, you rascal you, don't you swear;—

Dick. Why then in cool blood hear me speak to you. I tell you it's a city fortune I 'm about, she cares not a fig for your vartue, she 'll hear of nothing but quality.

She has quarrelled with one of her friends for having a better complexion, and is resolved she'll marry, to take place of her.

Mrs. Amlet. What a cherry-lip is there!

Dick. Therefore, good dear mother now, have a care and don't discover me; for if you do, all's lost.

Mrs. Amlet. Dear, dear, how thy fair bride will be delighted! Go, get thee gone, go! Go fetch her home! go fetch her home, I say!

Dick. Take care then of the main chance, my dear mother; remember if you discover me—

Mrs. Amlet. Go, fetch her home, I say!

Dick. You promise me then.

Mrs. Amlet. March!

Dick. But swear to me—

Mrs. Amlet. Begone, sirrah!

Dick. Well, I'll rely upon you—But one kiss before I go. *Kisses her heartily and runs off.*

Mrs. Amlet. Now the Lord love thee; for thou art a comfortable young man! *Exit.*

A Room in GRIPE'S *House.*

BRASS, FLIPPANTA. *Enter* DICK.

Dick. My dear Flippanta, how many thanks have I to pay thee!

Flippanta. Do you like her style?

Dick. The kindest little rogue! there's nothing but

she gives me leave to hope. I am the happiest man the world has in its care.

Flippanta. Not so happy as you think for neither, perhaps; you have a rival, sir, I can tell you that.

Dick. A rival!

Flippanta. Yes, and a dangerous one too.

Dick. Who, in the name of terror?

Flippanta. A devilish fellow; one Mr. Amlet.

Dick. Amlet! I know no such man.

Flippanta. You know the man's mother though; you met her here and are in her favour, I can tell you. If he worst you in your mistress, you shall e'en marry her, and disinherit him.

Dick. If I have no other rival but Mr. Amlet, I believe I shan't be much disturbed in my amour. But can't I see Corinna?

Flippanta. I don't know, she has always some of her masters with her: but I'll go see if she can spare you a moment, and bring you word. *Exit.*

Dick. I wish my old hobbling mother han't been blabbing something here she should not do.

Brass. Fear nothing, all's safe on that side yet. But how speaks young mistress's epistle? soft and tender?

Dick. As pen can write.

Brass. So you think all goes well there?

Dick. As my heart can wish.

Brass. You are sure on't?

Dick. Sure on't.

Brass. Why then, ceremony aside,
Putting on his hat.
You and I must have a little talk, Mr. Amlet.

Dick. Ah, Brass, what art thou going to do? Wou't ruin me?

Brass. Look you, Dick, few words; you are in a smooth way of making your fortune; I hope all will roll on. But how do you intend matters shall pass 'twixt you and me in this business?

Dick. Death and furies! What a time dost take to talk on 't!

Brass. Good words, or I betray you; they have already heard of one Mr. Amlet in the house.

Dick. Aside. Here 's a son . . . .

Brass. In short, look smooth, and be a good prince. I am your valet, 'tis true; your footman sometimes, which I 'm enraged at; but you have always had the ascendant, I confess. When we were schoolfellows, you made me carry your books, make your exercise, own your rogueries, and sometimes take a whipping for you. When we were fellow-prentices, though I was your senior, you made me open the shop, clean my master's shoes, cut last at dinner, and eat all the crust. Nay, in our punishments you still made good your post; for when once upon a time I was sentenced but to be whipped, I cannot deny but you were condemned to be hanged. So that in all times, I must confess, your inclinations have been greater and nobler than mine. However, I cannot consent that you should at once fix fortune for life, and I dwell in my humilities for the rest of my days.

Dick. Hark thee, Brass, if I do not most nobly by thee, I 'm a dog.

Brass. And when?

Dick. As soon as ever I am married.

Brass. Ah, the plague take thee!

Dick. Then you mistrust me?

Brass. I do, by my faith! Look you, sir, some folks we mistrust because we don't know 'em; others we mistrust because we do know 'em: and for one of these reasons I desire there may be a bargain beforehand. If not—*Raising his voice.* look ye, Dick Amlet!

Dick. Soft, my dear friend and companion.—*Aside.* The dog will ruin me!—*Aloud.* Say, what is't will content thee?

Brass. O ho!

Dick. But how canst thou be such a barbarian?

Brass. I learned it at Algiers.

Dick. Come, make thy Turkish demand then.

Brass. You know you gave me a bank bill this morning to receive for you.

Dick. I did so, of fifty pounds; 'tis thine. So, now thou art satisfied, all 's fixed.

Brass. It is not, indeed. There's a diamond necklace you robbed your mother of e'en now.

Dick. Ah, you Jew !

Brass. No words.

Dick. My dear Brass !

Brass. I insist.

Dick. My old friend !

Brass. Dick Amlet, *Raising his voice.* I insist.

Dick. Ah, the cormorant !—Well, 'tis thine : but thou 'lt never thrive with 't.

Brass. When I find it begins to do me mischief, I 'll give it you again. But I must have a wedding-suit.

Dick. Well.

Brass. Some good lace.

Dick. Thou shalt.

Brass. A stock of linen.

Dick. Enough.

Brass. Not yet ; a silver sword.

Dick. Well, thou shalt have that too. Now thou hast everything.

Brass. Heaven forgive me ! I forgot a ring of remembrance ; I would not forget all these favours for the world. A sparkling diamond will be always playing in my eye, and put me in mind of 'em.

Dick. Aside. This unconscionable rogue !—*Aloud.* Well, I 'll bespeak one for thee.

Brass. Brilliant ?

Dick. It shall. But if the thing don't succeed after all ?—

Brass. I 'm a man of honour and restore ; and so

the treaty being finished, I strike my flag of defiance, and fall into my respects again. *Taking off his hat.*

. . . .

A Room in GRIPE'S *House.*

CLARISSA, ARAMINTA, CORINNA, FLIPPANTA, Mrs. AMLET, BRASS.

Enter DICK AMLET.

Corinna. Look, look, Flippanta, here's the colonel come at last!

Dick. Ladies, I ask your pardon, I have stayed so long, but—

Mrs. Amlet. Ah, rogue's face, have I got thee, old Good-for-nought? Sirrah, sirrah, do you think to amuse me with your marriages, and your great fortunes? Thou hast played me a rare prank, by my conscience! Why, you ungracious rascal, what do you think will be the end of all this? Now Heaven forgive me, but I have a great mind to hang thee for 't.

Corinna. She talks to him very familiarly, Flippanta!

Flippanta. So methinks, by my faith!

Brass. Aside. Now the rogue's star is making an end of him.

Dick. Aside. What shall I do with her?

Mrs. Amlet. Do but look at him, my dames: he has the countenance of a cherubim, but he's a rogue in his heart.

Clarissa. What is the meaning of all this, Mrs. Amlet?

Mrs. Amlet. The meaning, good lack! Why this all-to-be-powdered rascal here is my son, an 't please you.—Ha, Graceless! Now I'll make you own your mother, vermin!

Clarissa. What, the colonel your son?

Mrs. Amlet. 'Tis Dick, madam, that rogue Dick I have so often told you of, with tears trickling down my old cheeks.

Araminta. The woman's mad, it can never be.

Mrs. Amlet. Speak, rogue, am I not thy mother, ha? Did I not bring thee forth? Say then.

Dick. What will you have me say? You had a mind to ruin me, and you have done 't; would you do any more?

Clarissa. Then, sir, you are son to good Mrs. Amlet?

Araminta. And have had the assurance to put upon us all this while!

Flippanta. And the confidence to think of marrying Corinna?

Brass. And the impudence to hire me for your servant, who am as well born as yourself?

Clarissa. Indeed I think he should be corrected.

Araminta. Indeed I think he deserves to be cudgelled.

Flippanta. Indeed I think he might be pumped.

Brass. Indeed I think he will be hanged.

Mrs. Amlet. Good lack-a-day! good lack-a-day! there's no need to be so smart upon him neither: if he is not a gentleman, he is a gentleman's fellow.—Come hither, Dick, they shan't run thee down neither; cock up thy hat, Dick, and tell 'em, though Mrs. Amlet is thy mother, she can make thee amends with ten thousand good pounds to buy thee some lands, and build thee a house in the midst on 't.

All. How!

Clarissa. Ten thousand pounds, Mrs. Amlet!

Mrs. Amlet. Yes forsooth, though I should lose the hundred you pawned your necklace for.—Tell 'em of that, Dick.

Corinna. Look you, Flippanta, I can hold no longer, and I hate to see the young man abused.—And so, sir, if you please, I'm your friend and servant, and what's mine is yours; and when our estates are put together, I don't doubt but we shall do as well as the best of 'em.

Dick. Sayest thou so, my little queen? Why then if dear mother will give us her blessing—

They kneel to Mrs. AMLET.

Mrs. Amlet. Ah-ha! ha! ha! ha! the pretty pair, the pretty pair! Rise, my chickens, rise, rise and face the proudest of 'em. And if madam does not deign to give her consent, a fig for her, Dick !—Why, how now?

Clarissa. Pray, Mrs. Amlet, don't be in a passion, the girl is my husband's girl, and if you can have his consent, upon my word you shall have mine, for anything belongs to him.

Flippanta. Then all's peace again, but we have been more lucky than wise.

COLLEY CIBBER

BORN 1671.   DIED 1757.

CIBBER's best service to the stage was his 'Apology for his Life,' the most entertaining and graphic record of the actors and actresses of a remarkable period that perhaps exists in any language. Cibber was a good actor, something of a fine gentleman, so far as fine clothes and foppish manners go to the 'make up' of that character. He was also one of the 'wits' of his time, and having the laws of stage-craft at his finger ends, and understanding the requirements of audiences, he was enabled to compound a successful comedy,' She wou'd and she wou'd not,' where the brisk give-and-take of the dialogue is borrowed from the dramatists of Charles II.'s age, and the bustling plot taken from a Spanish original. His comedies are the smart plays of a clever man whom circumstances, not natural genius, made a playwright. They do not quite possess the ring of true comedy.

COLLEY CIBBER

SHE WOU'D AND SHE WOU'D NOT

HYPOLITA, a young lady of a wilful and capricious humour, although she returns the affection of Don Philip, has treated him so disdainfully that he resolves to turn his thoughts from her, and to obey his father's commands to marry an unknown lady at Madrid,—for which city he starts at once.

Upon this Hypolita disguises herself and her maid Flora in male attire, and they follow him. On the journey they manage to obtain possession of Don Philip's portmanteau,—left behind by a careless servant,—and containing, along with money, jewels, and other valuables, his credentials to the father of his bride, Rosara. Armed with these documents, Hypolita determines to pass herself off as Don Philip, and to marry the lady herself, to prevent his doing so. On arriving at Madrid, Hypolita and Flora fall in with Trappanti, a former servant of Don Philip's, and Hypolita takes him into her service for the furthering of her scheme.

The complications caused by the appearance of two Don Philips—the false and the true one—end in the marriage of Don Philip with Hypolita, and of Rosara with Hypolita's brother, Octavio.

An Inn in Madrid.

Enter TRAPPANTI *alone, talking to himself.*

Indeed, my friend Trappanti, thou 'rt in a very thin condition; thou hast neither master, meat, nor money: not but, could'st thou part with that unappeasable itch of eating too, thou hast all the ragged virtues that were requisite to set up an ancient philosopher. Contempt and poverty, kicks, thumps, and thinking, thou hast endured with the best of them; but—when fortune turns thee up to hard fasting, that is to say, positively not eating at all, I perceive thou art a downright dunce, with the same stomach, and no more philosophy than a hound upon horse-flesh.—Fasting's the devil!—Let me see,—this, I take it, is the most frequented inn about Madrid, and if a keen guest or two should drop in now—Hark!

Host. Within. Take care of the gentlemen's horses there. See 'em well rubbed and littered.

Trappanti. Just alighted! If they do but stay to eat now! Impudence assist me; hah, a couple of pretty young sparks, faith!

Enter HYPOLITA *and* FLORA, *in men's habits. A Servant with a portmanteau.*

Trappanti. Welcome to Madrid, sir; welcome, sir.
Flora. Sir, your servant.
Servant. Have the horses pleased your honour?

Hypolita. Very well indeed, friend. Pr'ythee set down the portmanteau, and see that the poor creatures want nothing: they have performed well, and deserve our care.

Trappanti. I'll take care of that, sir. Here, ostler.
Exeunt TRAPPANTI *and Servant.*

. . . .

HYPOLITA, FLORA. *Enter* TRAPPANTI.

Hypolita. How now! what would this fellow have?

Trappanti. Servant, gentlemen; I have taken nice care of your nags; good cattle they are, by my troth, right and sound, I'll warrant 'em; they deserve care, and they have had it, and shall have it if they stay in this house—I always stand by, sir, see 'em rubbed down with my own eyes—Catch me trusting an ostler, I'll give you leave to fill for me, and drink for me too.

Flora. I have seen this fellow somewhere.

Trappanti. Hey-day! What, no cloth laid! Was ever such attendance! Hey, house! Tapster! Landlord! Hey! *Knocks.*
What was it you bespoke, gentlemen?

Hypolita. Really, sir, I ask your pardon. I have almost forgot you.

Trappanti. Pshah! dear Sir, never talk of it; I live here hard by—I have a lodging—I can't call it a lodging, neither;—that is, I have a—sometimes I am

I

here, and sometimes I am there, and so here and there one makes shift, you know.—Hey! Will these people never come? *Knocks.*

Hypolita. You give a very good account of yourself, sir.

Trappanti. Oh, nothing at all, Sir: Lord, Sir!—was it fish or flesh, sir?

Flora. Really, Sir, we have bespoke nothing yet.

Trappanti. Nothing! for shame! it's a sign you are young travellers. You don't know this house, Sir; why, they 'll let you starve if you don't stir, and call, and that like thunder too.—Hey! *Knocks.*

Hypolita. Ha, you eat here sometimes, I presume, Sir.

Trappanti. Umph!—Ay, Sir, that's as it happens—I seldom eat at home, indeed—Things are generally, you know, so out of order there, that—Did you hear any fresh news upon the road, Sir?

Hypolita. Only, sir, that the King of France lost a great horse-match upon the Alps, t' other day.

Trappanti. Hah, a very odd place for a horse-race—but the King of France may do anything.—Did you come that way, gentlemen, or—Hey! *Knocks.*

Enter Host.

Host. Did you call, gentlemen?

Trappanti. Yes, and bawl too, Sir. Here, the gentlemen are almost famished, and nobody comes near 'em. What have you in the house now, that will be ready presently?

Host. You may have what you please, Sir.

Hypolita. Can you get us a partridge?

Host. Sir, we have no partridges; but we'll get you what you please in a moment. We have a very good neck of mutton, Sir; if you please it shall be clapped down in a moment.

Hypolita. Have you no pigeons or chickens?

Host. Truly, Sir, we have no fowl in the house at present; if you please you may have anything else in a moment.

Hypolita. Then pr'ythee get us some young rabbits.

Host. Upon my word, Sir, rabbits are so scarce they are not to be had for money.

Flora. Have you any fish?

Host. Fish! Sir, I drest yesterday the finest dish that ever came upon a table; I am sorry we have none left, Sir; but, if you please, you may have anything else in a moment.

Trappanti. Plague on thee, hast thou nothing but anything-else in the house?

Host. Very good mutton, Sir.

Hypolita. Pr'ythee get us a breast, then.

Host. Breast! Don't you love the neck, Sir?

Hypolita. Ha' ye nothing in the house but the neck?

Host. Really, Sir, we don't use to be so unprovided, but at present we have nothing else left.

Trappanti. Faith, Sir, I don't know but a nothing-else may be very good meat, when anything-else is not to be had.

Hypolita. Then, pr'ythee, friend, let's have thy neck of mutton before that is gone too.

Trappanti. Sir, he shall lay it down this minute; I'll see it done. Gentlemen, I'll wait upon ye presently; for a minute I must beg your pardon and leave to lay the cloth myself.

Hypolita. By no means, Sir.

Trappanti. No ceremony, dear Sir; indeed I'll do it.

Exeunt Host and TRAPPANTI.

LOVE'S LAST SHIFT: OR THE FOOL IN FASHION

Two brothers named Worthy are frequent visitors at the house of Sir William Wisewou'd, a rich old gentleman, father to Narcissa and uncle to Hillaria. Sir William Wisewou'd designs to marry his daughter to the elder Worthy, who is possessed of a large estate, but the young man, though he pretends to enter into his views, is really in love with Hillaria. The younger Worthy is paying his addresses to Narcissa while Sir William Wisewou'd believes him to be acting on his brother's behalf; he also mediates between his brother and Hillaria, who has offended him by encouraging the attentions of an empty-headed fop, Sir Novelty Fashion. Amanda (the friend of Narcissa and Hillaria), a deserted and devoted wife, whose stratagem to reclaim her dissolute husband, Loveless, gives the play its name, succeeds in regaining his affections, and the brothers Worthy, after some difficulties about the ladies' fortunes, obtain the hands of Hillaria and Narcissa.

A Garden belonging to Sir WILLIAM WISEWOU'D'S House.

Enter NARCISSA, HILLARIA, and Sir NOVELTY FASHION.

Hillaria. Oh! for heaven's sake! no more of this gallantry, Sir Novelty: for I know you say the same to every woman you see.

Sir Novelty. Every one that sees you, Madam, must say the same. Your beauty, like the rack, forces every beholder to confess his crime—of daring to adore you.

Narcissa. Aside. Oh! I han't patience to hear all this. If he be blind I'll open his eyes. *Aloud.* I vow, Sir Novelty, you men of amour are strange creatures : you think no woman worth your while, unless you walk over a rival's ruin to her heart : I know nothing has encouraged your passion to my cousin more than her engagement to Mr. Worthy.

Hillaria. Aside. Poor creature! Now is she angry she han't the addresses of a fop I nauseate.

Sir Novelty. Oh, Madam! as to that I hope the lady will easily distinguish the sincerity of her adorers. Though I must allow, Mr. Worthy is infinitely the handsomer person.

Narcissa. Oh fie! Sir Novelty, make not such a preposterous comparison.

Sir Novelty. Oh, Gad! Madam, there's no comparison.

Narcissa. Pardon me, Sir, he's an unpolished animal.

Sir Novelty. Why, does your ladyship really think me tolerable?

Hillaria. Aside. So! She has snapt his heart already.

Sir Novelty. Pray, Madam, how do I look to-day?—What, cursedly? I'll warrant;—I don't know, Madam:—'Tis true—the town does talk of me indeed;—but the devil take me, in my mind, I am a very ugly fellow.

Narcissa. Now you are too severe, Sir Novelty.

Sir Novelty. Not I, burn me:—for heaven's sake, deal freely with me, Madam;—and if you can, tell me—one tolerable thing about me.

Hillaria. Aside. 'Twould pose me, I'm sure.

Narcissa. Oh, Sir Novelty! this is unanswerable; 'tis hard to know the brightest part of a diamond.

Sir Novelty. You'll make me blush, stop my vitals, Madam.—*Aside.* Egad, I always said she was a woman of sense. Strike me dumb, I am in love with her.—I'll try her farther. *Aloud.* But, Madam, is it possible I may vie with Mr. Worthy?—Not that he is a rival of mine, Madam; for I can assure you, my inclinations lie where, perhaps, your ladyship little thinks.

Hillaria. Aside. So! now I am rid of him.

Sir Novelty. But pray tell me, Madam : for I really love a severe critick : I am sure you must believe he has a more happy genius in dress : for my part, I am but a sloven.

Narcissa. He is a genius unsufferable! Why he dresses worse than a captain of the militia : but you, Sir Novelty, are a true original, the very pink of fashion : I'll warrant you there's not a milliner in town but has got an estate by you.

Sir Novelty. I must confess, Madam, I am for doing good to my country : for you see this suit, Madam— I suppose you are not ignorant what a hard time the ribband weavers have had since the late mourning : now my design is to set the poor rogues up again, by recommending this sort of trimming, the fancy is pretty well for second mourning.—By the way, Madam, I had fifteen hundred guineas laid in my hand, as a gratuity to encourage it : but i'gad I refused them, being too well acquainted with the consequence of taking a bribe in a national concern.

Hillaria. A very charitable fashion, indeed, Sir Novelty! But how if it should not take?

Narcissa. Ridiculous! Take! I warrant you in a week the whole town will have it; though perhaps Mr. Worthy will be one of the last of them: he's a mere Valet de Chambre to all fashions ; and never is in any till his betters have left them off.

Sir Novelty. Nay, Gad, now I must laugh; for the devil take me if I did not meet him, not above a fortnight ago, in a coat with buttons no bigger than nutmegs.

Hillaria. There, I must confess, you out-do him, Sir Novelty.

Sir Novelty. Oh, dear Madam, why mine are not above three inches diameter.

Hillaria. But methinks, Sir Novelty, your sleeve is a little too extravagant.

Sir Novelty. Nay, Madam, there you wrong me; mine does but reach my knuckles, but my Lord Overdo's cover his diamond ring.

Hillaria. Nay, I confess the fashion may be very useful to you gentlemen that make campaigns: for should you unfortunately lose an arm, or so, that sleeve might be very convenient to hide the defect on 't.

Sir Novelty. Hah! I think your ladyship's in the right on 't, Madam.   *Hiding his hand in his sleeve.*

Narcissa. Oh! such an air! so becoming a negligence—Upon my soul, Sir Novelty, you'll be the envy of the *beau-monde.*

Hillaria. Mr. Worthy! a good fancy were thrown away upon him; but you, sir, are an ornament to your clothes.

Sir Novelty. Then your ladyship really thinks they are—*bien entendus?*

Hillaria. A *merveille, Monsieur.*

Sir Novelty. Aside. She has almost as much wit as

her cousin. *Aloud.* I must confess, Madam, this coat has had an universal approbation; for this morning I had all the most eminent taylors in town at my levee, earnestly petitioning for the first measure of it: now, Madam, if you thought it would oblige Mr. Worthy, I would let his taylor have it before any of them.

Narcissa. See, here he comes, and the deuce take me, I think it would be a great piece of good-nature; for I declare he looks as rough as a Dutch corporal. —Prithee, Sir Novelty, let's laugh at him.

Sir Novelty. O Gad! no, Madam, that were too cruel: why, you know he can't help it.—Let's take no notice of him.

Hillaria. Aside. Wretched coxcomb!

Enter WORTHY.

Worthy. Aside. I find my resolution is but vain, my feet have brought me hither against my will: but sure I can command my tongue, which I'll bite off ere it shall seek a reconciliation. Still so familiar there! But 'tis no matter, I'll try if I can wear indifference, and seem as careless in my love as she is of her honour, which she can never truly know the worth of, while she persists to let a fool thus play with it. *Aloud.* Ladies, your humble servant.

Hillaria. Aside. Now I can't forbear fretting his spleen a little. *Aloud.* Oh, Mr. Worthy! we are admiring Sir Novelty and his new suit. Did you ever see so sweet a fancy? He is as full of variety as a good play.

Worthy. He's a very pleasant comedy, indeed, Madam; and dressed with a great deal of good satire; and, no doubt, may oblige both the stage and the town, especially the ladies.

Hillaria. Aside. So! There's for me—

Sir Novelty. O Gad! Nay, pr'ythee, Tom, you know my humour—Ladies (stop my vitals) I don't believe there are five hundred in town that ever took any notice of me.

Worthy. Oh, sir, there are some that take so much notice of you, that the town takes notice of them for 't.

Sir Novelty. How of them, Tom, upon my account? O Gad, I wou'd not be the ruin of any lady's reputation, for the world. Stop my vitals, I'm very sorry for 't. Pr'ythee name but one that has a favourable thought of me, and to convince you that I have no design upon her, I'll instantly visit her in an unpowdered periwig.

Young WORTHY, *Sir* NOVELTY FASHION, NARCISSA.

Young Worthy. To Sir NOVELTY, *who is taking snuff.* Pray give me leave to beg a word in private with you, Sir, if you please.

Sir Novelty. Ay, Sir, with all my heart.

Young Worthy. Sir—

Sir Novelty. Nay; 'tis right, I'll assure you.

Offering his box.

Young Worthy. Ay, sir—but now the lady wou'd be alone.

Sir Novelty. Sir.

Young Worthy. The lady would be alone, sir.

Sir Novelty. I don't hear her say any such thing.

Young Worthy. Then I tell you so, and I would advise you to believe me.

Sir Novelty. I shall not take your advice, Sir: but if you really think the lady would be alone, why—you had best leave her.

Young Worthy. In short, Sir, your company is very unseasonable just at present.

Sir Novelty. I can tell you, Sir, if you have no more wit than manners, the lady will be but scurvily entertained.

Narcissa. Oh, fie, gentlemen! no quarrelling before a woman, I beseech you. Pray let me know the business.

Sir Novelty. My business is love, Madam.

Narcissa. And yours, Sir?

Young Worthy. What I hope you are no stranger to, Madam. As for that spark, you need take no care of him: for if he stays much longer, I will do his business myself.

Narcissa. Aside. Well, I vow, love's a pleasant thing, when the men come to cutting of throats once. O Gad! I'd fain have them fight a little—Methinks Narcissa would sound so great in an expiring lover's mouth—Well, I am resolved Sir Novelty shall not go yet; for I will have the pleasure of hearing myself praised a little; though I don't marry this month for't. *Aloud.* Come, gentlemen, since you both say love's your business, e'en plead for yourselves; and he that speaks the greatest passion shall have the fairest return.

Young Worthy. Aside. Oh, the devil! now is she rapt with the hopes of a little flattery. There's no remedy but patience. 'Sdeath! What a piece have I to work upon!

Narcissa. Come, gentlemen, one at a time. Sir Novelty, what have you to say to me?

Sir Novelty. In the first place, Madam, I was the first person in England that was complimented with the name of beau, which is a title I prefer before right honourable, for that may be inherited; but this I extorted from the whole nation, by my surprising mien, and unexampled gallantry.

Narcissa. So, Sir.

Sir Novelty. Then another thing, Madam: it has been observed that I have been eminently successful in those fashions I have recommended to the town; and I don't question but this very suit will raise as many ribband-weavers as ever the clipping or melting trade did goldsmiths.

Narcissa. Aside. Pish! What does the fool mean! He says nothing of me yet.

Sir Novelty. In short, madam, the cravat-string, the garter, the sword-knot, the centurine, the stein-kirk, the large button, the long sleeve, the plume, and full peruke, were all created, cry'd down, or revived by me; in a word, Madam, there has never been anything particularly taking or agreeable for these ten years past, but your humble servant was the author of it.

Young Worthy. Aside. Where the devil will this end?

Narcissa. This is all extravagant, Sir Novelty: but what have you to say to me, Sir?

Sir Novelty. I'll come to you presently, Madam, I have just done: then you must know, my coach and equipage are as well known as myself; and since the conveniency of two play-houses, I have a better opportunity of shewing them; for between every act—Whisk—I am gone from one to the other: Oh! what pleasure 'tis, at a good play, to get out before half an act's done!

Narcissa. Why at a good play?

Sir Novelty. O, Madam, it looks particular and gives the whole audience an opportunity of turning upon me at once: then do they conclude I have some extraordinary business, or a fine woman to go to at least: and then again, it shows my contempt of what the dull town think their chief diversion. But if I do stay a play out, I always sit with my back to the stage.

Narcissa. Why so, Sir?

Sir Novelty. Then every one will imagine I have been tired with it before: or that I am jealous who talks to who in the King's box. And thus, Madam, do I take more pains to preserve a public reputation, than ever any lady took, after the small-pox, to recover her complexion.

Narcissa. Well, but to the point. What have you to say to me, Sir Novelty?

Young Worthy. Aside. Now does she expect some compliment shall out-flatter her glass.

Sir Novelty. To you, Madam?—Why, I have been saying all this to you.

Narcissa. To what end, Sir?

Sir Novelty. Why, all this I have done for your sake.

Narcissa. What kindness is it to me?

Sir Novelty. Why, Madam, don't you think it more glory to be beloved by one eminently particular person, whom all the town knows and talks of, than to be adored by five hundred dull souls that have lived *incognito*?

Narcissa. That, I must confess, is a prevailing argument; but still you ha'n't told me why you love me.

Young Worthy. That's a task he has left for me, Madam.

Sir Novelty. 'Tis a province I never undertake, I

must confess : I think 'tis sufficient, if I tell a lady why she should love me.

Narcissa. Aside. Hang him ! he's too conceited : he's so in love with himself, he won't allow a woman the bare comfort of a cold compliment. *Aloud.* Well, Mr. Worthy.

Young Worthy. Why, Madam, I have observed several particular qualities in your Ladyship, that I have perfectly adored you for ; as the majestic toss of your head ;—your obliging low courtesy ;—your satirical smile ;—your blushing laugh ;—your demure look ;— the careless tie of your hood ;—the genteel flirt of your fan ;—the designed accident in your letting it fall, and your agreeable manner of receiving it from him that takes it up.

> *What he speaks, she imitates in dumb show.*
> *They both offer to take up her fan,*
> *and, in striving, Young* WORTHY
> *pushes Sir* NOVELTY *on his back.*

Sir Novelty. Adjusting himself. I hope your ladyship will excuse my disorder, Madam.

CONGREVE

BORN 1670.   DIED 1729.

What makes CONGREVE hold so high a place among comic dramatists is not so much that naturalness which is the distinguishing characteristic of his school, nor his insight, nor his breadth; it is his style that gives him his pre-eminence, that 'subtle turn and heightening' which makes the sentences of his dialogue shine like well-faceted precious stones. The polish and elaboration he gives would be excessive were his wit less hard and pure and bright. Congreve has numerous obvious drawbacks, his outlook is not a broad one upon human nature, but upon 'the town' only—his sympathies are narrow, his morality on the wrong side of tolerable. A more technical objection to him as a playwright is that there is too much ingenuity, too much complexity, and too little true art in his plots; they do not move us, and they hardly interest us. Nevertheless, there are qualifications in Congreve for a great, almost the greatest, place in our literature as a comic dramatist besides this one of consummate wit and consummate style. One of these is his marvellous faculty of characterization. Mirabell, the fine gentleman lover, is not the mere 'walking gentleman' of most playwrights, but manly, lover-like, ready-spoken, and most witty on occasion. Lady Wishfort, Mincing, Foible, Lord Froth, the coxcomb, and that most entertaining of sots and country louts, Sir Wilfull Witwoud, are all personages with the stamp of humanity upon them, and Millamant is by common consent the most delightful of fine ladies that the world has ever known. Congreve's supremacy in the domain of comedy is to a great extent due to this, that he was an accomplished fine gentleman in the first place, and an accomplished *littérateur* in the second. Voltaire is said to have snubbed him for taking credit to himself in the first character only, and subsequent critics have approved the snub. Yet it may have been no coxcombry at all in Congreve, but only a true gentleman's modesty, and equivalent to saying, 'Do not praise me for my literary talent when I do but repeat in my days the wit and manners of the society I live in, and in my verse I only reproduce the ease and epigrams of the wits, my friends.' Of course he did much more than this. No society talk was ever so clever as that of Congreve's *dramatis personæ*: his very dullards are brighter in speech than most authors' wits, and no fine lady, even at the Court of Queen Anne, could ever have been so airy, so graceful, so wayward, so brilliant, and so charming as Millamant.

CONGREVE

THE WAY OF THE WORLD

MIRABELL is in love with Millamant, an affected fine lady, who returns his affection. Half her fortune will be forfeited if she marries without the consent of her aunt and guardian, old Lady Wishfort, who has planned her marriage with her cousin, Sir Wilfull Witwoud, a coarse country lout, Lady Wishfort's nephew, who has just come up from the country, and is about to travel. His half-brother, Witwoud, a flippant London fop and fool, is another admirer of Millamant's.

Mirabell causes Waitwell, his valet (secretly married to Foible, Lady Wishfort's maid), to personate Sir Rowland, Mirabell's uncle, and offer marriage to Lady Wishfort, intending to threaten to expose her folly unless she withdraws her opposition to his suit. The false Sir Rowland, however, is discovered in time, and Lady Wishfort turns upon Foible for her complicity in the plot. Mirabell then offers, on condition of Lady Wishfort's consenting to his marriage with Millamant, to save the gravely compromised fortune of Lady Wishfort's daughter, Mrs. Fainall, whose husband, Fainall, has quarrelled with her. This he is able to do; Foible is forgiven, and all ends happily.

A Chocolate House.

MIRABELL, FAINALL, BETTY *the Waitress, and* WITWOUD.

Witwoud. Afford me your compassion, my dears! pity me, Fainall! Mirabell, pity me!

Mirabell. I do from my soul.

Fainall. Why, what's the matter?

Witwoud. No letters for me, Betty?

Betty. Did not a messenger bring you one but now, sir?

Witwoud. Ay, but no other?

Betty. No, sir.

Witwoud. That's hard, that's very hard—A messenger! a mule, a beast of burden! he has brought me a letter from the fool my brother, as heavy as a panegyric in a funeral sermon, or a copy of commendatory verses from one poet to another: and what's worse, 'tis as sure a forerunner of the author, as an epistle dedicatory.

Mirabell. A fool, and your brother, Witwoud?

Witwoud. Ay, ay, my half-brother. My half-brother he is, no nearer upon honour.

Mirabell. Then 'tis possible he may be but half a fool.

Witwoud. Good, good, Mirabell, le drole! good, good; hang him, don't let's talk of him. . . . Mirabell?

Mirabell. Ay.

Witwoud. My dear, I ask ten thousand pardons; —gad, I have forgot what I was going to say to you !
Mirabell. I thank you heartily, heartily.
Witwoud. No, but prithee excuse me :—my memory is such a memory.
Mirabell. Have a care of such apologies, Witwoud; for I never knew a fool but he affected to complain, either of the spleen or his memory.
Fainall. What have you done with Petulant?
Witwoud. He's reckoning his money—my money it was.—I have no luck to-day.
Fainall. You may allow him to win of you at play : for you are sure to be too hard for him at repartee ; since you monopolise the wit that is between you, the fortune must be his of course.
Mirabell. I don't find that Petulant confesses the superiority of wit to be your talent, Witwoud.
Witwoud. Come, come, you are malicious now and would breed debates.—Petulant's my friend, and a very honest fellow, and a very pretty fellow, and has a smattering—faith and troth, a pretty deal of an odd sort of a small wit : nay, I'll do him justice. I'm his friend, I won't wrong him neither.—And if he had any judgment in the world, he would not be altogether contemptible. Come, come, don't detract from the merits of my friend.
Fainall. You don't take your friend to be over-nicely bred?
Witwoud. No, no, hang him, the rogue has no

manners at all, that I must own :—no more breeding than a bum-bailiff, that I grant you :—'tis pity, faith ; the fellow has fire and life.

Mirabell. What, courage ?

Witwoud. Hum, faith I don't know as to that, I can't say as to that—Yes, faith, in a controversy, he'll contradict anybody.

Mirabell. Though 'twere a man whom he feared, or a woman whom he loved.

Witwoud. Well, well, he does not always think before he speaks ;—we have all our failings : you are too hard upon him, you are, faith. Let me excuse him—I can defend most of his faults, except one or two : one he has, that's the truth on't ; if he were my brother, I could not acquit him :—that, indeed, I could wish were otherwise.

Mirabell. Ay marry, what's that, Witwoud ?

Witwoud. O, pardon me !—expose the infirmities of my friend !—No, my dear, excuse me there.

Fainall. What, I warrant he's insincere, or 'tis some such trifle.

Witwoud. No, no ; what if he be ? 'tis no matter for that, his wit will excuse that : a wit should no more be sincere, than a woman constant ; one argues a decay of parts, as t' other of beauty.

Mirabell. May be you think him too positive ?

Witwoud. No, no ; his being positive is an incentive to argument, and keeps up conversation.

Fainall. Too illiterate?

Witwoud. That! that's his happiness:—his want of learning gives him the more opportunities to show his natural parts.

Mirabell. He wants words?

Witwoud. Ay: but I like him for that now; for his want of words gives me very often the pleasure to explain his meaning.

Fainall. He's impudent?

Witwoud. No, that's not it.

Mirabell. Vain?

Witwoud. No.

Mirabell. What! he speaks unseasonable truths sometimes, because he has not wit enough to invent an evasion?

Witwoud. Truths! ha! ha! ha! no, no; since you will have it,—I mean, he never speaks truth at all—that's all. He will lie like a chambermaid, or a woman of quality's porter. Now that's a fault.

MIRABELL, Mrs. FAINALL, Mrs. MILLAMANT, WITWOUD, *and* MINCING.

Mirabell. Here she comes, i' faith, full sail, with her fan spread and her streamers out, and a shoal of fools for tenders; ha, no, I cry her mercy!

Mrs. Fainall. I see but one poor empty sculler; and he tows her woman after him.

Mirabell. To MILLAMANT. You seem to be unattended, madam—you used to have the *beau monde* throng after you; and a flock of gay fine perukes hovering round you.

Witwoud. Like moths about a candle.—I had like to have lost my comparison for want of breath.

Millamant. O I have denied myself airs to-day, I have walked as fast through the crowd.

Witwoud. As a favourite just disgraced; and with as few followers.

Millamant. Dear Mr. Witwoud, truce with your similitudes; for I am as sick of 'em—

Witwoud. As a physician of a good air. I cannot help it, madam, though 'tis against myself.

Millamant. Yet again!—Mincing, stand between me and his wit.

Witwoud. Do, Mrs. Mincing, like a screen before a great fire.—I confess I do blaze to-day, I am too bright.

Mrs. Fainall. But, dear Millamant, why were you so long?

Millamant. Long! Lord, have I not made violent haste; I have asked every living thing I met for you; I have enquired after you, as after a new fashion.

Witwoud. Madam! truce with your similitudes.—No, you met her husband, and did not ask him for her.

Millamant. By your leave, Witwoud, that were like enquiring for an old fashion, to ask a husband for his wife.

Witwoud. Hum, a hit! a hit! a palpable hit! I confess it.

Mrs. Fainall. You were dressed before I came abroad.

Millamant. Ay, that's true.—O but then I had—Mincing, what had I? Why was I so long?

Mincing. O mem, your laship stayed to peruse a packet of letters.

Millamant. O ay, letters—I had letters—I am persecuted with letters—I hate letters—Nobody knows how to write letters, and yet one has 'em, one does not know why. They serve one to pin up one's hair.

Witwoud. Is that the way? Pray, madam, do you pin up your hair with all your letters? I find I must keep copies.

Millamant. Only with those in verse, Mr. Witwoud; I never pin up my hair with prose.—I think I tried once, Mincing.

Mincing. O mem, I shall never forget it.

Millamant. Ay, poor Mincing tift and tift all the morning.

Mincing. Till I had the cramp in my fingers, I'll vow, mem: and all to no purpose. But when your laship pins it up with poetry, it sits so pleasant the next day as anything, and is so pure and so crips.

Witwoud. Indeed, so crips?

Mincing. You're such a critic, Mr. Witwoud.

Mrs. MILLAMANT *and* MIRABELL.

Mirabell. I would beg a little private audience, too. —You had the tyranny to deny me last night; though you knew I came to impart a secret to you that concerned my love.

Millamant. You saw I was engaged.

Mirabell. Unkind! You had the leisure to entertain a herd of fools; things who visit you from their excessive idleness; bestowing on your easiness that time which is the incumbrance of their lives. How can you find delight in such society? It is impossible they should admire you, they are not capable: or if they were, it should be to you as a mortification; for sure to please a fool is some degree of folly.

Millamant. I please myself:—besides, sometimes to converse with fools is for my health.

Mirabell. Your health! Is there a worse disease than the conversation of fools?

Millamant. Yes, the vapours; fools are physic for it, next to assafœtida.

Mirabell. You are not in a course of fools?

Millamant. Mirabell, if you persist in this offensive freedom, you'll displease me.—I think I must resolve, after all, not to have you:—we shan't agree.

Mirabell. Not in our physic, it may be.

Millamant. And yet our distemper, in all likelihood.

will be the same ; for we shall be sick of one another. I shan't endure to be reprimanded nor instructed ; 'tis so dull to act always by advice, and so tedious to be told of one's faults—I can't bear it. Well, I won't have you, Mirabell—I'm resolved—I think—you may go. —Ha! ha! ha! what would you give, that you could help loving me?

Mirabell. I would give something that you did not know I could not help it.

Millamant. Come, don't look grave then. Well, what do you say to me?

Mirabell. I say that a man may as soon make a friend by his wit, or a fortune by his honesty, as win a woman with plain-dealing and sincerity.

Millamant. Sententious Mirabell!—Prithee don't look with that violent and inflexible wise face, like Solomon at the dividing of the child in an old tapestry hanging.

Mirabell. You are merry, madam, but I would persuade you for a moment to be serious.

Millamant. What, with that face ? no, if you keep your countenance, 'tis impossible I should hold mine. Well, after all, there is something very moving in a love-sick face. Ha! ha! ha!—well, I won't laugh, don't be peevish—Heigho! now I'll be melancholy, as melancholy as a watch-light. Well, Mirabell, if ever you will win me woo me now.—Nay, if you are so tedious, fare you well ;—I see they are walking away.

Mirabell. Can you not find in the variety of your disposition one moment—

Millamant. To hear you tell me Foible's married, and your plot like to speed;—no.

Mirabell. But how came you to know it?

Millamant. Without the help of the devil, you can't imagine; unless she should tell me herself. Which of the two it may have been, I will leave you to consider; and when you have done thinking of that, think of me.

Exit.

Sir WILFULL *drunk. Lady* WISHFORT, WITWOUD, MILLAMANT, *and Mrs.* FAINALL.

Lady Wishfort. Out upon 't, out upon 't! At years of discretion and comport yourself at this rantipole rate!

Sir Wilfull. No offence, aunt.

Lady Wishfort. Offence! as I'm a person, I'm ashamed of you—foh! how you stink of wine! D'ye think my niece will ever endure such a Borachio? you're an absolute Borachio.

Sir Wilfull. Borachio?

Lady Wishfort. At a time when you should commence an amour and put your best foot foremost—

Sir Wilfull. 'S heart, an you grutch me your liquor, make a bill—give me more drink and take my purse.—

Sings.

> *Prithee fill me the glass,*
> *Till it laugh in my face,*
> *With ale that is potent and mellow;*
> *He that whines for a lass*
> *Is an ignorant ass,*
> *For a bumper has not its fellow.*

But if you would have me marry my cousin—say the word, and I'll do't—Wilfull will do't, that's the word—Wilfull will do't, that's my crest—my motto I have forgot.

Lady Wishfort. My nephew's a little overtaken, cousin—but 'tis with drinking your health.—O' my word, you are obliged to him.

Sir Wilfull. *In vino veritas,* aunt.—If I drunk your health to-day, cousin—I am a Borachio. But if you have a mind to be married, say the word and send for the piper; Wilfull will do't. If not, dust it away, and let's have t'other round.—Tony!—Odds heart, where's Tony!—Tony's an honest fellow, but he spits after a bumper, and that's a fault. *Sings.*

> *We'll drink and we'll never ha' done, boys,*
> *Put the glass then around with the sun, boys,*
> *Let Apollo's example invite us;*
> *For he's drunk every night,*
> *And that makes him so bright,*
> *That he's able next morning to light us.*

The sun's a good pimple, an honest soaker; he has a

cellar at your Antipodes. If I travel, aunt, I touch at your Antipodes.—Your Antipodes are a good, rascally sort of topsy-turvy fellows : if I had a bumper, I'd stand upon my head and drink a health to 'em.—A match or no match, cousin, with the hard name?—Aunt, Wilfull will do 't. . . . .

Millamant. Your pardon, madam, I can stay no longer—sir Wilfull grows very powerful. Eh! how he smells! I shall be overcome if I stay.—Come, cousin. *Exit.*

Lady Wishfort. Smells! he would poison a tallow-chandler and his family! Beastly creature, I know not what to do with him!—Travel, quotha! ay, travel, travel, get thee gone, get thee gone, get thee but far enough, to the Saracens, or the Tartars, or the Turks!—for thou art not fit to live in a Christian commonwealth, thou beastly Pagan!

Sir Wilfull. Turks, no ; no Turks, aunt : your Turks are infidels and believe not in the grape. Your Mahometan, your Mussulman is a dry stinkard—no offence, aunt. My map says that your Turk is not so honest a man as your Christian. I cannot find by the map that your Mufti is orthodox—whereby it is a plain case that orthodox is a hard word, aunt, and (*Hiccups.*) Greek for claret.— *Sings.*

To drink is a Christian diversion,
Unknown to the Turk or the Persian:

*Let Mahometan fools
Live by heathenish rules
And be damn'd over tea-cups and coffee,
But let British lads sing,
Crown a health to the king,
And a fig for your sultan and sophy!*

Ah Tony ! . . . lead on, little Tony—I 'll follow thee, my Anthony, my Tantony, sirrah, thou shalt be my Tantony, and I 'll be thy pig. *Sings.*

And a fig for your sultan and sophy!

Exeunt Sir WILFULL and WITWOUD.

Lady Wishfort. This will never do. It will never make a match—at least before he has been abroad.

A Room in Lady WISHFORT'S House.

Lady WISHFORT and FOIBLE.

Lady Wishfort. Out of my house, out of my house, thou viper ! thou serpent, that I have fostered ! thou bosom traitress that I raised from nothing !—Begone ! begone ! begone !—go ! go !—That I took from washing of old gauze and weaving of dead hair, with a bleak, blue nose over a chafing-dish of starved embers, and dining behind a traverse rag, in a shop no bigger than a birdcage !—go, go ! starve again, do, do !

Foible. Dear madam, I 'll beg pardon on my knees.

Lady Wishfort. Away ! out ! out !—Go, set up for yourself again !—Do, drive a trade, do, with your three-pennyworth of small ware, flaunting upon a pack-thread, under a brandy-seller's bulk, or against a dead wall by a ballad-monger! Go, hang out an old Frisoneer gorget, with a yard of yellow colbertine again! Do; an old gnawed mask, two rows of pins and a child's fiddle; a glass necklace with the beads broken, and a quilted nightcap with one ear! go, go, drive a trade!—These were your commodities, you treacherous trull! this was the merchandise you dealt in when I took you into my house, placed you next myself, and made you governante of my whole family! You have forgot this, have you, now you have feathered your nest?

Foible. No, no, dear madam. Do but hear me, have but a moment's patience, I'll confess all. Mr. Mirabell seduced me; I am not the first that he has wheedled with his dissembling tongue; your ladyship's own wisdom has been deluded by him; then how should I, a poor ignorant, defend myself? O madam, if you knew but what he promised me, and how he assured me your ladyship should come to no damage!—Or else the wealth of the Indies should not have bribed me to conspire against so good, so sweet, so kind a lady as you have been to me.

Lady Wishfort. No damage! What, to betray me, and marry me to a cast-servingman! No damage! O thou frontless impudence!

Foible. Pray do but hear me, madam; he could not marry your ladyship, madam.—No, indeed, his marriage was to have been void in law, for he was married to me first, to secure your ladyship. Yes, indeed, I inquired of the law before I would meddle or make.

Lady Wishfort. What then, I have been your property, have I? I have been convenient to you, it seems!—This exceeds all precedent; I am brought to fine uses, to become a botcher of second-hand marriages between Abigails and Andrews!—you and your Philander!—I'll Duke's-place you, as I am a person! Your turtle is in custody already: you shall coo in the same cage, if there be a constable or warrant in the parish. *Exit.*

Foible. Oh that ever I was born! Oh that I was ever married!—A bride!—ay, I shall be a Bridewell-bride.—Oh!

THE DOUBLE DEALER.

THE plot of this play is made up of intrigues and counter-intrigues of great complexity, relieved by the humours and affectations of Lord and Lady Froth and Mr. Brisk. The scene is laid at the house of Lord Touchwood, uncle to Mellefont, who is engaged to marry Cynthia, daughter of Sir Paul Plyant. Lord Froth is a man of fashion and a solemn coxcomb; Mr. Brisk is a pert one. Lady Froth is 'a great coquette and pretender to poetry, wit, and learning.' Careless is Mellefont's friend and confidant, of a blunt, down-right temper.

A Gallery in Lord TOUCHWOOD'S *House, with Chambers adjoining.*

Enter CARELESS, *crossing the stage, with his hat, gloves, and sword in his hands, as just risen from table;* MELLEFONT *following him.*

Mellefont. Ned, Ned, whither so fast? what, turned flincher? Why, you won't leave us?

Careless. Where are the women? I'm weary of guzzling, and begin to think them the better company.

Mellefont. Then thy reason staggers, and thou 'rt almost drunk.

Careless. No, faith, but your fools grow noisy; and if a man must endure the noise of words without sense, I think the women have more musical voices, and become nonsense better.

Mellefont. Why, they are at the end of the gallery, retired to their tea and scandal, according to their ancient custom, after dinner. . . .

The Same. Lord TOUCHWOOD, *Lord* FROTH, *Sir* PAUL PLYANT, *and* BRISK.

Lord Touchwood. Out upon 't, nephew!—leave your father-in-law and me to maintain our ground against young people!

Mellefont. I beg your lordship's pardon; we were just returning.

Sir Paul Plyant. Were you, son? gadsbud, much better as it is.—Good, strange! I swear I'm almost tipsy—t' other bottle would have been too powerful for me,—as sure as can be it would.—We wanted your company; but Mr. Brisk—where is he? I swear and vow he's a most facetious person,—and the best company.—And, my Lord Froth, your lordship is so merry a man, he! he! he!

Lord Froth. O foy, Sir Paul! what do you mean? Merry! O barbarous! I'd as lieve you call'd me fool.

Sir Paul Plyant. Nay, I protest and vow now, 'tis true; when Mr. Brisk jokes, your lordship's laugh does so become you, he! he! he!

Lord Froth. Ridiculous! Sir Paul, you're strangely mistaken, I find champagne is powerful. I assure you, Sir Paul, I laugh at nobody's jest but my own or a lady's; I assure you, Sir Paul.

Brisk How? how, my lord? what, affront my wit! let me perish, do I never say anything worthy to be laughed at?

Lord Froth. O foy! don't misapprehend me, I don't say so, for I often smile at your conceptions. But there is nothing more unbecoming a man of quality than to laugh; 'tis such a vulgar expression of the passion! everybody can laugh. Then, especially to laugh at the jest of an inferior person, or when anybody else of the same quality does not laugh with one; ridiculous!

To be pleased with what pleases the crowd! Now when I laugh, I always laugh alone.

Brisk. I suppose, that's because you laugh at your own jests, egad, ha! ha! ha!

Lord Froth. He! he! I swear, though, your raillery provokes me to a smile.

Brisk. Ay, my lord, 'tis a sign I hit you in the teeth if you show 'em.

Lord Froth. He! he! he! I swear that's so very pretty, I can't forbear.

Careless. I find a quibble bears more sway in your lordship's face than a jest.

Lord Touchwood. Sir Paul, if you please we'll retire to the ladies, and drink a dish of tea, to settle our heads.

Sir Paul. With all my heart.—Mr. Brisk, you'll come to us,—or call me when you joke; I'll be ready to laugh incontinently.

Exeunt Lord TOUCHWOOD *and
Sir* PAUL PLYANT.

Enter MELLEFONT, CARELESS, *Lord* FROTH, *and*
BRISK.

Mellefont. But does your lordship never see comedies?

Lord Froth. O yes, sometimes;—but I never laugh.

Mellefont. No!

Lord Froth. O no ;—never laugh indeed, sir.

Careless. No! why, what d' ye go there for?

Lord Froth. To distinguish myself from the commonalty, and mortify the poets : the fellows grow so conceited when any of their foolish wit prevails upon the side-boxes,—I swear—he! he! he! I've often restrained my inclinations to laugh,—he! he! he! to avoid giving them encouragement.

Mellefont. You are cruel to yourself, my lord, as well as malicious to them.

Lord Froth. I confess I did myself some violence at first ; but now I think I have conquered it.

Brisk. Let me perish, my lord, but there is something very particular in the humour! 'Tis true, it makes against wit, and I'm sorry for some friends of mine that write, but, egad, I love to be malicious. Nay, deuse take me, there's wit in 't too : and wit must be foiled by wit ; cut a diamond with a diamond ; no other way, egad!

Lord Froth. O, I thought you would not be long before you found out the wit.

Careless. Wit! in what? where the devil's the wit in not laughing when a man has a mind to 't?

Brisk. O Lord, why, can't you find it out?—Why, there 'tis, in the not laughing ;—don't you apprehend me? *Aside to* FROTH. My lord, Careless is a very honest fellow, but harkee,—you understand me, somewhat heavy, a little shallow, or so.—*Aloud.* Why,

I'll tell you now. Suppose now you come up to me —nay, prithee, Careless, be instructed—suppose, as I was saying, you come up to me holding your sides, and laughing, as if you would—Well—I look grave, and ask the cause of this immoderate mirth—you laugh on still, and are not able to tell me.—Still I look grave and not so much as smile.

Careless. Smile! no; what the devil should you smile at, when you suppose I can't tell you?

Brisk. Pshaw! pshaw! prithee, don't interrupt me. —But I tell you, you shall tell me—at last—but it shall be a great while first.

Careless. Well, but prithee don't let it be a great while, because I long to have it over.

Brisk. Well, then, you tell me some good jest, or very witty thing, laughing all the while as if you were ready to die, and I hear it, and look thus.—Would not you be disappointed?

Careless. No; for if it were a witty thing, I should not expect you to understand it.

Lord Froth. O foy, Mr. Careless! all the world allows Mr. Brisk to have wit; my wife says he has a great deal. I hope you think her a judge.

Brisk. Pooh, my lord, his voice goes for nothing! I can't tell how to make him apprehend. *To* CARE-LESS. Take it t' other way:—Suppose I say a witty thing to you?

Careless. Then I shall be disappointed indeed.

Mellefont. Let him alone, Brisk; he is obstinately bent not to be instructed.

Brisk. I'm sorry for him, the deuse take me!

Mellefont. Shall we go to the ladies, my lord?

Lord Froth. With all my heart; methinks we are a solitude without 'em.

Mellefont. Or, what say you to another bottle of champagne?

Lord Froth. O, for the universe, not a drop more, I beseech you!—Oh intemperate! I have a flushing in my face already.

Takes out a pocket-glass, and looks in it.

Brisk. Let me see, let me see, my lord! I broke my glass that was in the lid of my snuff-box. Hum! deuse take me, I have encouraged a pimple here too.

Takes the glass, and looks.

Lord Froth. Then you must mortify him with a patch; my wife shall supply you. Come, gentlemen, *allons,* here is company coming.

. . . .

The Gallery in Lord TOUCHWOOD'S *House.*

Lady FROTH *and* CYNTHIA.

Cynthia. Indeed, madam! Is it possible your ladyship could have been so much in love?

Lady Froth. I could not sleep; I did not sleep one wink for three weeks together.

Cynthia. Prodigious ! I wonder want of sleep, and so much love, and so much wit as your ladyship has, did not turn your brain.

Lady Froth. O my dear Cynthia, you must not rally your friend.—But really, as you say, I wonder too ;—but then I had a way : for between you and I, I had whimsies and vapours, but I gave them vent.

Cynthia. How pray, madam?

Lady Froth. O I writ, writ abundantly;—do you never write?

Cynthia. Write what?

Lady Froth. Songs, elegies, satires, encomiums, panegyrics, lampoons, plays, or heroic poems.

Cynthia. O Lord, not I, madam ; I'm content to be a courteous reader.

Lady Froth. O inconsistent ! in love, and not write ! if my lord and I had been both of your temper, we had never come together.—O bless me ! what a sad thing that would have been, if my lord and I should never have met !

Cynthia. Then neither my lord nor you would ever have met with your match, on my conscience.

Lady Froth. O' my conscience, no more we should ; thou sayest right : for sure my Lord Froth is as fine a gentleman and as much a man of quality ! Ah, nothing at all of the common air !—I think I may say he wants nothing but a blue ribbon and a star to make him shine, the very phosphorus of our hemisphere. Do you understand those two hard words? if you don't, I'll explain 'em to you.

Cynthia. Yes, yes, madam, I'm not so ignorant. —*Aside.* At least I won't own it, to be troubled with your instructions.

Lady Froth. Nay, I beg your pardon; but being derived from the Greek, I thought you might have escaped the etymology.—But I'm the more amazed to find you a woman of letters, and not write! Bless me! how can Mellefont believe you love him?

Cynthia. Why faith, madam, he that won't take my word shall never have it under my hand.

Lady Froth. I vow Mellefont's a pretty gentleman, but methinks he wants a manner.

Cynthia. A manner! What's that, madam?

Lady Froth. Some distinguishing quality, as for example, the *bel air* or *brillant* of Mr. Brisk; the solemnity yet complaisance of my lord, or something of his own that should look a little *je ne sai quoi;* he is too much a mediocrity, in my mind.

Cynthia. He does not indeed affect either pertness or formality, for which I like him. Here he comes.

Lady Froth. And my lord with him; pray, observe the difference.

Enter Lord FROTH, MELLEFONT, *and* BRISK.

Cynthia. Aside. Impertinent creature! I could almost be angry with her now.

Lady Froth. My lord, I have been telling Cynthia how much I have been in love with you, I swear I have; I'm not ashamed to own it now. Ah, it makes my heart leap! I vow, I sigh when I think on 't; my dear lord, ha! ha! ha! do you remember, my lord? *Squeezes him by the hand, looks kindly on him, and then laughs out.*

Lord Froth. Pleasant creature! perfectly well.—Ah, that look! ay, there it is! who could resist? 'twas so my heart was made a captive first, and ever since 't has been in love with happy slavery.

Lady Froth. O that tongue! that dear, deceitful tongue! that charming softness in your mien and your expression! and then your bow! Good, my lord, bow as you did when I gave you my picture: here, suppose this my picture. *Gives him a pocket-glass.* Pray mind, my lord; ah, he bows charmingly!— Nay, my lord, you shan't kiss it so much, I shall grow jealous, I vow now.

He bows profoundly low, then kisses the glass.

Lord Froth. I saw myself there, and kissed it for your sake.

Lady Froth. Ah, gallantry to the last degree!—Mr. Brisk, you're a judge; was ever anything so well bred as my lord?

Brisk. Never anything but your ladyship, let me perish!

Lady Froth. Oh, prettily turned again! let me die

but you have a great deal of wit!—Mr. Mellefont, don't you think Mr. Brisk has a world of wit?

Mellefont. O yes, madam.

Brisk. O dear, madam.

Lady Froth. An infinite deal?

Brisk. O heavens, madam!—

Lady Froth. More wit than anybody?

Brisk. I'm everlastingly your humble servant, deuse take me, madam.

Lord Froth. To CYNTHIA. Don't you think us a happy couple?

Cynthia. I vow, my lord, I think you the happiest couple in the world; for you're not only happy in one another and when you are together, but happy in yourselves, and by yourselves.

Lord Froth. I hope Mellefont will make a good husband too.

Cynthia. 'Tis my interest to believe he will, my lord.

Lord Froth. D'ye think he'll love you as well as I do my wife? I'm afraid not.

Cynthia. I believe he'll love me better.

Lord Froth. Heavens! that can never be; but why do you think so?

Cynthia. Because he has not so much reason to be fond of himself.

Lord Froth. Oh, your humble servant for that, dear madam.—Well, Mellefont, you'll be a happy creature,

Mellefont. Ay, my lord, I shall have the same reason for my happiness that your lordship has, I shall think myself happy.

Lord Froth. Ah, that's all.

Brisk. To Lady FROTH. Your ladyship's in the right; but, egad, I'm wholly turned into satire. I confess I write but seldom, but when I do—keen iambics, egad! But my lord was telling me, your ladyship has made an essay toward an heroic poem.

Lady Froth. Did my lord tell you? yes, I vow, and the subject is my lord's love to me. And what do you think I call it? I dare swear you won't guess—*The Syllabub;* ha! ha! ha!

Brisk. Because my lord's title's Froth, egad; ha! ha! ha! deuse take me, very *à propos* and surprising, ha! ha! ha!

Lady Froth. He! ay, is not it?—And then I call my lord Spumoso, and myself—what d'ye think I call myself?

Brisk. Lactilla, may be:—'gad, I cannot tell.

Lady Froth. Biddy, that's all; just my own name.

Brisk. Biddy! egad, very pretty! Deuse take me, if your ladyship has not the art of surprising the most naturally in the world!—I hope you'll make me happy in communicating the poem.

Lady Froth. O you must be my confidant, I must ask your advice.

Brisk. I'm your humble servant, let me perish !—I presume your ladyship has read Bossu?

Lady Froth. O yes, and Rapin, and Dacier upon Aristotle and Horace.

. . . .

CYNTHIA, Lord FROTH, Lady FROTH, *and* BRISK.

Lady Froth. Then you think that episode between Susan, the dairy-maid, and our coachman, is not amiss ; you know I may suppose the dairy in town as well as in the country.

Brisk. Incomparable, let me perish !—But then being an heroic poem, had not you better call him a charioteer? charioteer sounds great; besides, your ladyship's coachman having a red face, and you comparing him to the sun ; and you know the sun is called heaven's charioteer.

Lady Froth. Oh, infinitely better! I am extremely beholden to you for the hint; stay, we'll read over those half a score lines again.   *Pulls out a paper.* Let me see here, you know what goes before,—the comparison, you know.   *Reads.*

For as the sun shines every day,
So, of our coachman I may say—

Brisk. I'm afraid that simile won't do in wet weather ;—because you say the sun shines every day.

Lady Froth. No, for the sun it won't, but it will do

for the coachman; for you know there's most occasion for a coach in wet weather.

Brisk. Right, right, that saves all.

Lady Froth. Then, I don't say the sun shines all the day, but that he peeps now and then; yet he does shine all the day too, you know, though we don't see him.

Brisk. Right, but the vulgar will never comprehend that.

Lady Froth. Well, you shall hear. Let me see.
Reads.

> *For as the sun shines every day,*
> *So, of our coachman I may say,*
> *He shows his drunken fiery face,*
> *Just as the sun does, more or less.*

Brisk. That's right, all's well, all's well!—*More or less.*

Lady Froth. Reads. *And when at night his labour's done,*
Then too, like heaven's charioteer the sun—

Ay, *charioteer* does better.

> *Into the dairy he descends.*
> *And there his whipping and his driving ends;*
> *There he's secure from danger of a bilk,*
> *His fare is paid him, and he sets in milk.*

For Susan, you know, is Thetis, and so—

Brisk. Incomparably well and proper, egad !—But I have one exception to make :—don't you think *bilk* (I know it's good rhyme), but don't you think *bilk* and *fare* too like a hackney-coachman ?

Lady Froth. I swear and vow, I am afraid so.— And yet our Jehu was a hackney-coachman when my lord took him.

Brisk. Was he? I'm answered, if Jehu was a hackney-coachman.—You may put that in the marginal notes though, to prevent criticism.—Only mark it with a small asterism, and say, *Jehu was formerly a hackney-coachman.*

Lady Froth. I will; you'd oblige me extremely to write notes to the whole poem.

Brisk. With all my heart and soul, and proud of the vast honour, let me perish !

Lord Froth. Hee ! hee ! hee ! my dear, have you done?—won't you join with us? We were laughing at my Lady Whifler and Mr. Sneer.

Lady Froth. Ay, my dear.—Were you? O filthy Mr. Sneer ! he's a nauseous figure, a most fulsamic fop, foh ! He spent two days together in going about Covent-Garden, to suit the lining of his coach with his complexion. . . . Then that t' other great strapping lady—I can't hit of her name—the old fat fool that paints so exorbitantly.

Brisk. I know whom you mean—but, deuse take me ! I can't hit of her name neither.—Paints, d'ye say? why she lays it on with a trowel. . . .

Lady Froth. Oh, you made a song upon her, Mr. Brisk.

Brisk. He! egad, so I did:—my lord can sing it.

Cynthia. O, good my lord, let's hear it.

Brisk. 'Tis not a song neither;—it's a sort of an epigram, or rather an epigrammatic sonnet; I don't know what to call it, but it's satire. Sing it, my lord.

Lord Froth. Sings. Ancient Phyllis has young graces,
  'Tis a strange thing, but a true one;
   Shall I tell you how?
  She herself makes her own faces,
  And each morning wears a new one;
   Where's the wonder now?

Brisk. Short, but there's salt in't; my way of writing, egad!

ADDISON

BORN 1672.   DIED 1719.

It is one of the wonders of literature that ADDISON with a wit so keen, a literary touch so delicate, and a fertility of fancy so great, should have failed as a comedy-writer. Macaulay, noting how the 'Roger de Coverley' papers work into a charming narrative, regrets that a writer so capable of invaluable character-fiction should never have attempted a true novel. Addison's comedy, 'The Drummer,' written with probably some help from Steele, goes some way, though not the whole way, to induce us to think that this regret was groundless. The 'Drummer' has in places a humour of its own, but were its authorship unknown few critics probably would detect in its scenes the masterly touch and refined taste of Addison. It was perhaps the moralizing tendency of the author and the age that make this comedy wanting in the right comedy flavour.

ADDISON

THE DRUMMER, OR THE HAUNTED HOUSE

THE country house of Lady Truman, whose husband, Sir George Truman, is reported to have fallen in battle in the Netherlands fourteen months before, is haunted by an invisible drummer, supposed to be Sir George's ghost. Lady Truman has dismissed one suitor, Mr. Fantome, and is amusing herself at the expense of another, Mr. Tinsel, a coxcomb and fortune-hunter. The mysterious drummer is Fantome, who with the connivance of Abigail, Lady Truman's elderly and shrewish waiting-woman, conceals himself in a hidden closet dressed as Sir George, with the object of suddenly appearing before his rival Tinsel, and frightening him from the house. Meanwhile Sir George, who has not been killed, but kept a close prisoner, on his release writes privately to Vellum, his steward, a formal, precise old man, and, anxious to test his wife's conduct, comes to the house as a conjuror, to lay the supposed ghost. Tinsel having been scared away by Fantome, as the drummer, Fantome himself quits the house on the appearance of Sir George without his disguise, and the play ends with the happy reunion of Sir George and Lady Truman and the marriage of Vellum with Abigail.

A great Hall.

Enter the Butler, Coachman, and Gardener.

Butler. There came another coach to town last night, that brought a gentleman to enquire about this strange noise we hear in the house. This spirit will bring a power of custom to the George—If so be he continues his pranks, I design to sell a pot of ale, and set up the sign of the drum.

Coachman. I'll give madam warning, that's flat— I've always lived in sober families—I'll not disparage myself to be a servant in a house that's haunted.

Gardener. I'll e'en marry Nell, and rent a bit of ground of my own, if both of you leave madam; not but that madam's a very good woman—if Mrs. Abigail did not spoil her—Come, here's her health.

Butler. 'Tis a very hard thing to be a butler in a house that is disturbed. He made such a racket in the cellar, last night, that I'm afraid he'll sour all the beer in my barrels.

Coachman. Why then, John, we ought to take it off as fast as we can—Here's to you—He rattled so loud under the tiles, last night, that I verily thought the house would have fallen over our heads. I durst not go up into the cock-loft this morning, if I had not got one of the maids to go along with me.

Gardener. I thought I heard him in one of my bedposts. I marvel, John, how he gets into the house, when all the gates are shut.

Butler. Why, look ye, Peter, your spirit will creep you into an augre-hole—he'll whisk ye through a keyhole, without so much as justling against one of the wards.

Coachman. Poor Madam is mainly frightened, that's certain, and verily believes it is my master, that was killed in the last campaign.

Butler. Out of all manner of question, Robin, 'tis Sir George. Mrs. Abigail is of opinion, it can be none but his honour. He always loved the wars; and, you know, was mightily pleased, from a child, with the music of a drum.

Gardener. I wonder his body was never found after the battle.

Butler. Found! why, ye fool, is not his body here about the house? Dost thou think he can beat his drum without hands and arms?

Coachman. 'Tis master, as sure as I stand here alive; and I verily believe I saw him last night in the town-close.

Gardener. Ay! How did he appear?

Coachman. Like a white horse.

Butler. Phoo, Robin! I tell ye, he has never appeared yet, but in the shape of the sound of a drum.

Coachman. This makes one almost afraid of one's own shadow. As I was walking from the stable, t' other night, without my lanthorn, I fell across a beam, that lay in my way; and faith, my heart was in my mouth. I thought I had stumbled over a spirit.

Butler. Thou might'st as well have stumbled over a straw. Why, a spirit is such a little thing, that I have heard a man, who was a great scholar, say, that he'll dance ye a Lancashire hornpipe upon the point of a needle. . . . My lady must have him laid, that's certain, whatever it cost her.

Gardener. Faith, I could tell you one way to drive him off.

Coachman. How's that?

Gardener. I'll tell you immediately.—*Drinks.*—I fancy Mrs. Abigail might scold him out of the house.

Coachman. Ay, she has a tongue that would drown his drum, if anything would.

Butler. Pugh, this is all froth; you understand nothing of the matter. The next time it makes a noise, I tell you what ought to be done—I would have the steward speak Latin to it.

Coachman. Ay, that would do, if the steward had but courage.

Gardener. There you have it. He's a fearful man. If I had as much learning as he, and I met the ghost, I'd tell him his own. But, alack! what can one of us poor men do with a spirit, that can neither write nor read?

Butler. Thou art always cracking and boasting, Peter; thou dost not know what mischief it might do thee, if such a silly dog as thee should offer to speak to it. For aught I know, he might flea thee alive, and make parchment of thy skin, to cover his drum with.

Gardener. A fiddlestick! tell not me—I fear nothing, not I; I never did harm in my life; I never committed murder.

Butler. I verily believe thee. Keep thy temper, Peter; after supper we'll drink each of us a double mug, and then let come what will.

Gardener. Why, that's well said, John—An honest man, that is not quite sober, has nothing to fear— Here's to ye—Why, now if he should come this minute, here would I stand—Ha! what noise is that?

Butler and Coachman. Ha! Where?

Gardener. The devil! the devil! Oh, no; 'tis Mrs. Abigail.

Butler. Ay, faith! 'tis she; 'tis Mrs. Abigail! A good mistake; 'tis Mrs. Abigail.

Enter ABIGAIL.

Abignil. Here are your drunken sots for you! Is this a time to be guzzling, when gentry are come to the house! Why don't you lay your cloth? How come you out of the stables? Why are you not at work in your garden?

Gardener. Why, yonder's the fine Londoner and madam fetching a walk together; and, methought, they looked as if they should say they had rather have my room than my company.

Butler. And so, forsooth, being all three met together, we are doing our endeavours to drink this same drummer out of our heads.

Gardener. For you must know, Mrs. Abigail, we are all of opinion that one can't be a match for him, unless one be as drunk as a drum.

Coachman. I am resolved to give madam warning to hire herself another coachman; for I came to serve my master, d'ye see, while he was alive: but do suppose that he has no further occasion for a coach, now he walks.

Butler. Truly, Mrs. Abigail, I must needs say, that this same spirit is a very odd sort of a body, after all, to fright madam, and his old servants, at this rate.

Gardener. And truly, Mrs. Abigail, I must needs say, I served my master contentedly, while he was living; but I will serve no man living (that is, no man that is not living) without double wages.

Abigail. Ay, 'tis such cowards as you that go about with idle stories, to disgrace the house, and bring so many strangers about it: you first frighten yourselves, and then your neighbours.

Gardener. Frightened! I scorn your words: frightened quoth-a!

Abigail. What, you sot, are you grown pot-valiant?

Gardener. Frightened with a drum! that's a good

one! It will do us no harm, I'll answer for it: it will bring no bloodshed along with it, take my word. It sounds as like a train-band drum as ever I heard in my life.

Butler. Pr'ythee, Peter, don't be so presumptuous.

Abigail. Aside. Well, these drunken rogues take it as I could wish.

Gardener. I scorn to be frightened, now I'm in for 't; if old dub-a-dub should come into the room, I would take him—

Butler. Pr'ythee, hold thy tongue.

Gardener. I would take him—

The drum beats: the Gardener endeavours to get off, and falls.

Butler and Coachman. Speak to it, Mrs. Abigail.

Gardener. Spare my life, and take all I have.

Coachman. Make off, make off, good butler; and let us go hide ourselves in the cellar.

They all run off.

Abigail. Alone. So, now the coast is clear, I may venture to call out my drummer.—But first let me shut the door lest we be surprised. Mr. Fantome, Mr. Fantome! *He beats.* Nay, nay, pray come out: the enemy's fled—I must speak with you immediately—Don't stay to beat a parley.

The back scene opens, and discovers FANTOME *with a drum.*

FARQUHAR

Born 1678.   Died 1707.

FARQUHAR is perhaps inferior, but not by much, in the qualities of good dialogue to Congreve, Wycherley, and Vanbrugh. There is not, to my thinking, quite the same high quality of comedy in his utterance. He is less high-bred, but he is as sprightly as, and more good-natured than any of them. He had travelled, served in the army, and seen more than the narrow world of coffee-houses and theatres. He extended the list of the comic dramatic personages of the day, and his Captain Plume, the fine gentleman officer, Boniface, the innkeeper, Cherry, his lively daughter, Scrub, the country servant who guesses they are talking of *him*, 'for they laughed consumedly,' and above all the inimitable recruiting officer, Sergeant Pike—are all invaluable additions to our stock of comedy characters. His plots are simpler and better than those of his brother playwrights, they have more life and movement, and the episodes succeed each other in an unforced way which must have made his pieces very pleasant to audiences. The excellent scene quoted from the 'Recruiting Officer' is very characteristic of this author's heartiness and rollicking humour. It seems drawn from the life, and tradition says that Captain Plume was none other than Captain Farquhar himself.

The scene from the 'Inconstant'—also here quoted—affords an excellent example of the true comic treatment of a very strong 'situation,' as opposed to its melodramatic treatment. There may be a little sacrifice of truth to nature in Mirabell's light-heartedness while he is in the hands of the bravoes, and in his humorous turning of the tables upon them afterwards when the rescue comes, but there is more than a compensating gain in genuine comedy, and, over and above the comedy, there is a touch of genuine human feeling which never comes amiss.

FARQUHAR

THE BEAUX' STRATAGEM

AIMWELL and his friend Archer are two young gentlemen whom lack of funds has caused to leave London under pretence of going to Brussels. They arrive at Lichfield, Archer passing for Aimwell's footman, and put up at an inn kept by Boniface and his daughter Cherry, intending by a judicious expenditure of their last two hundred pounds to attract the notice of some country heiress.

Aimwell is soon remarked by Dorinda, daughter of Lady Bountiful, and sister-in-law of Mrs. Sullen. She sends Scrub, their servant, to discover who he is, but he can obtain no information about him. After many adventures Aimwell succeeds in marrying Dorinda, and Archer weds Mrs. Sullen, who gets divorced from her drunken and brutal husband, Squire Sullen.

A Room in BONIFACE'S *Inn.*

Enter BONIFACE, *running.*

Boniface. Chamberlain! maid! Cherry! daughter Cherry! all asleep? all dead?

Enter CHERRY, *running.*

Cherry. Here, here! why d' ye bawl so, father? d' ye think we have no ears?

Boniface. You deserve to have none, you young minx! The company of the Warrington coach has stood in the hall this hour, and nobody to show them to their chambers.

Cherry. And let 'em wait, father; there's neither red-coat in the coach nor footman behind it.

Boniface. But they threaten to go to another inn to-night.

Cherry. That they dare not, for fear the coachman should overturn them to-morrow.—Coming! coming!—Here's the London coach arrived.

Enter Coach-passengers, with trunks, bandboxes, and other luggage, and cross the stage.

Boniface. Welcome, ladies!

Cherry. Very welcome, gentlemen! Chamberlain, show the Lion and the Rose.

Exit with the company.

Enter AIMWELL and ARCHER, the latter carrying a portmanteau.

Boniface. This way, this way, gentlemen.

Aimwell. *To ARCHER.* Set down the things; go to the stable, and see my horses well rubbed.

Archer. I shall, sir. *Exit.*

Aimwell. You're my landlord, I suppose?

Boniface. Yes, sir, I'm old Will Boniface, pretty well known upon this road, as the saying is.

Aimwell. O Mr. Boniface, your servant !

Boniface. O sir !—What will your honour please to drink, as the saying is ?

Aimwell. I have heard your town of Lichfield much famed for ale ; I think I 'll taste that.

Boniface. Sir, I have now in my cellar ten tun of the best ale in Staffordshire ; 'tis smooth as oil, sweet as milk, clear as amber, and strong as brandy; and will be just fourteen year old the fifth day of next March, old style.

Aimwell. You 're very exact, I find, in the age of your ale.

Boniface. As punctual, sir, as I am in the age of my children. I 'll show you such ale !—Here, tapster, broach number 1706, as the saying is.—Sir, you shall taste my *Anno Domini.*—I have lived in Lichfield, man and boy, above eight-and-fifty years, and, I believe, have not consumed eight-and-fifty ounces of meat.

Aimwell. At a meal, you mean, if one may guess your sense by your bulk.

Boniface. Not in my life, sir, I have fed purely upon ale; I have eat my ale, drank my ale, and I always sleep upon ale.

Enter Tapster with a bottle and glass, and exit.

Now, sir, you shall see !   *Pours out a glass.*
Your worship's health.—Ha ! delicious, delicious !

fancy it burgundy, only fancy it, and 'tis worth ten shillings a quart.

Aimwell. Drinks. 'Tis confounded strong!

Boniface. Strong! it must be so, or how should we be strong that drink it?

Aimwell. And have you lived so long upon this ale, landlord?

Boniface. Eight-and-fifty years, upon my credit, sir—but it killed my wife, poor woman, as the saying is.

Aimwell. How came that to pass?

Boniface. I don't know how, sir; she would not let the ale take its natural course, sir; she was for qualifying it every now and then with a dram, as the saying is; and an honest gentleman that came this way from Ireland, made her a present of a dozen bottles of usquebaugh—but the poor woman was never well after: but howe'er, I was obliged to the gentleman, you know.

Aimwell. Why, was it the usquebaugh that killed her?

Boniface. My Lady Bountiful said so. She, good lady, did what could be done; she cured her of three tympanies, but the fourth carried her off. But she's happy and I'm contented, as the saying is.

Aimwell. Who's that Lady Bountiful you mentioned?

Boniface. Ods my life, sir, we'll drink her health. —*Drinks.* My Lady Bountiful is one of the best of women. Her last husband, Sir Charles Bountiful, left her worth a thousand pound a year; and, I believe, she lays out one-half on 't in charitable uses for the good of her neighbours: . . . . in short she has cured more people in and about Lichfield in ten years than the doctors have killed in twenty; and that's a bold word.

. . . .

The Gallery in Lady BOUNTIFUL'S *House.*

Mrs. SULLEN *and* DORINDA. *Enter* SCRUB.

Dorinda. Well, Scrub, what news of the gentleman?

Scrub. Madam, I have brought you a packet of news.

Dorinda. Open it quickly, come.

Scrub. In the first place I enquired who the gentleman was; they told me he was a stranger. Secondly, I asked what the gentleman was; they answered and said, that they never saw him before. Thirdly, I enquired what countryman he was; they replied 'twas more than they knew. Fourthly, I demanded whence he came; their answer was, they could not tell. And, fifthly, I asked whither he went; and they replied they knew nothing of the matter,—and this is all I could learn.

Mrs. Sullen. But what do the people say? Can't they guess?

Scrub. Why, some think he's a spy, some guess he's a mountebank, some say one thing, some another; but for my own part, I believe he's a Jesuit.

Dorinda. A Jesuit! why a Jesuit?

Scrub. Because he always keeps his horses ready saddled, and his footman talks French.

Mrs. Sullen. His footman!

Scrub. Ay, he and the count's footman were gabbering French like two ducks in a mill-pond; and I believe they talked of me, for they laughed consumedly.

Dorinda. What sort of livery has the footman?

Scrub. Livery! Lord, madam, I took him for a captain, he's so bedizzened with lace! And then he has tops to his shoes, up to his mid leg, a silver-headed cane dangling at his knuckles; he carries his hands in his pockets just so— *Walks about foppishly.* and has a fine long periwig tied up in a bag.—Lord, madam, he's clear another sort of man than I.

Mrs. Sullen. That may easily be.

THE INCONSTANT; OR, THE WAY TO WIN HIM

MIRABEL is of a wild, roving disposition. He has just returned from travelling abroad, and refuses to marry Oriana, his father's ward, to whom he is betrothed, and plans going abroad again. Oriana disguises herself and enters his service as a page, unrecognized by him. Mirabel makes the acquaintance of Mrs. Lamorce, an adventuress, and calling at her house attended only by his supposed page, finds himself in the hands of four bravoes—whom, however, he affects to believe to be gentlemen. As a last hope of escape, he sends the page on a pretended errand for wine, who, seeing Mirabel's danger, fetches his friend Captain Duretete and a guard of soldiers. The bravoes are arrested, and Mirabel, full of gratitude to the page, desires him to ask what reward he will. Oriana discovers herself and claims the fulfilment of his contract to her, which Mirabel gladly promises.

LAMORCE'S Lodgings.

MIRABEL. *Enter* LAMORCE *and Four Bravoes.*

Mirabel. Starts back. Hum ! hum ! *Aside.* Murdered, murdered to be sure!—Nobody near me!—These cut-throats make always sure work.—What shall I do? I have but one way.—*Aloud.* Are these gentlemen your relations, madam ?

Lamorce. Yes, sir.

Mirabel. Gentlemen, your most humble servant !—Sir, your most faithful !—Yours, sir, with all my heart !—Your most obedient !— *Salutes all round.* No ceremony—next the lady—pray, sir. *They all sit.*

Lamorce. Well, sir, and how d' ye like my friends?

Mirabel. O madam, the most finished gentlemen ! I was never more happy in good company in my life. —I suppose, sir, you have travelled ?

First Bravo. Yes, sir.

Mirabel. Which way, may I presume?

First Bravo. In a western barge, sir.

Mirabel. Ha! ha! ha! very pretty; facetious pretty gentleman!

Lamorce. Ha! ha! ha! Sir, you have got the prettiest ring upon your finger there—

Mirabel. Ah, madam! 'tis at your service with all my heart. *Offering the ring.*

Lamorce. By no means, sir, a family-ring!
Takes it.

Mirabel. No matter, madam.—*Aside.* Seven hundred pound, by this light!

Second Bravo. Pray, sir, what's o'clock?

Mirabel. Hum! Sir, I forgot my watch at home.

Second Bravo. I thought I saw the string of it just now.

Mirabel. Ods my life, sir, I beg your pardon! Here it is—but it don't go. *Putting it up.*

Lamorce. O dear sir, an English watch! Tompion's, I presume?

Mirabel. D' ye like it, madam? No ceremony.—
LAMORCE *takes the watch.*
'Tis at your service with all my heart and soul.—*Aside.* Tompion's! hang ye.

First Bravo. But, sir, above all things, I admire the fashion and make of your sword-hilt.

Mirabel. I'm mighty glad you like it, sir.

First Bravo. Will you part with it, sir?

Mirabel. Sir, I won't sell it.
First Bravo. Not sell it, sir !
Mirabel. No, gentlemen—but I'll bestow it with all my heart. *Offering it.*
First Bravo. O sir, we shall rob you !
Mirabel. Aside. That you do, I'll be sworn !— *Aloud.* I have another at home, pray, sir.—

Gives his sword.

Gentlemen, you're too modest ; have I anything else that you fancy ? *To First Bravo.* Sir, will you do me a favour ? I am extremely in love with that wig which you wear, will you do me the favour to change with me?

First Bravo. Look'ee, sir, this is a family-wig, and I will not part with it, but if you like it—

Mirabel. Sir, your most humble servant.

They change wigs.

First Bravo. Madam, your most humble slave.

Goes up foppishly to LAMORCE *and salutes her.*

Second Bravo. Aside. The fellow's very liberal, shall we murder him ?

First Bravo. Aside. What ! let him 'scape to hang us all, and I to lose my wig ! no, no. I want but a handsome pretence to quarrel with him, for you know we must act like gentlemen. *Aloud.* Here, some wine !

Enter Servant, with wine.

Sir, your good health. *Pulls* MIRABEL *by the nose.*

Mirabel. O sir, your most humble servant! A pleasant frolic enough, to drink a man's health, and pull him by the nose; ha! ha! ha! the pleasantest pretty humoured gentleman!

Lamorce. Help the gentleman to a glass.

MIRABEL drinks.

First Bravo. How d' ye like the wine, sir?

Mirabel. Very good o' the kind, sir; but I'll tell ye what, I find we're all inclined to be frolicsome, and egad, for my own part, I was never more disposed to be merry; let's make a night on 't, ha!—This wine is pretty, but I have such burgundy at home!—Look'ee, gentlemen, let me send for a dozen flasks of my burgundy, I defy France to match it.—'Twill make us all life, all air; pray, gentlemen.

Second Bravo. Eh! shall us have his burgundy?

First Bravo. Yes, faith, we'll have all we can. Here, call up the gentleman's servant. *Exit Servant.* What think you, Lamorce?

Lamorce. Yes, yes.—Your servant is a foolish country boy, sir, he understands nothing but innocence?

Mirabel. Ay, ay, madam. Here, page.—

Enter ORIANA.

Take this key, and go to my butler; order him to send half-a-dozen flasks of the red burgundy, marked a thousand, and be sure you make haste, I long to entertain my friends here, my very good friends

All. Ah, dear sir!

First Bravo. Here, child, take a glass of wine. Your master and I have changed wigs, honey, in a frolic. Where had you this pretty boy, honest Mustapha?

Oriana. Aside. Mustapha!

Mirabel. Out of Picardy.—This is the first errand he has made for me, and if he does it right, I'll encourage him.

Oriana. The red burgundy, sir?

Mirabel. The red, marked a thousand, and be sure you make haste.

Oriana. I shall, sir. *Exit.*

First Bravo. Sir, you were pleased to like my wig, have you any fancy for my coat? Look'ee, sir, it has served a great many honest gentlemen very faithfully.

Mirabel. Not so faithfully, for I'm afraid it has got a scurvy trick of leaving all its masters in necessity. *Aside.* The insolence of these dogs is beyond their cruelty.

Lamorce. You're melancholy, sir!

Mirabel. Only concerned, madam, that I should have no servant here but this little boy.—He'll make some confounded blunder, I'll lay my life on't; I would not be disappointed of my wine for the universe.

Lamorce. He'll do well enough, sir; but supper's ready, will you please to eat a bit, sir?

Mirabel. O madam, I never had a better stomach in my life.

Lamorce. Come then; we have nothing but a plate of soup.   *Exit MIRABEL, handing LAMORCE.*

Second Bravo. That wig won't fall to your share.

First Bravo. No, no, we'll settle that after supper; in the meantime the gentleman shall wear it.

Second Bravo. Shall we despatch him?

Third Bravo. To be sure: I think he knows me.

First Bravo. Ay, ay, dead men tell no tales. I wonder at the impudence of the English rogues, that will hazard the meeting a man at the bar that they have encountered upon the road. I han't the confidence to look a man in the face after I have done him an injury; therefore we'll murder him.   *Exeunt.*

Mirabel. Bloody hell-hounds, I overheard you! Was I not two hours ago the happy, gay, rejoicing Mirabel? How did I plume my hopes in a fair coming prospect of a long scene of years! Life courted me with all the charms of vigour, youth, and fortune; and to be torn away from all my promised joys, is more than death; the manner too—by villains.—O my Oriana, this very moment might have blessed me in thy arms! and my poor boy, the innocent boy!— Confusion!—But hush, they come; I must dissemble.

Enter Bravoes.

Still no news of my wine, gentlemen?

First Bravo. No, sir, I believe your country booby has lost himself, and we can wait no longer for 't.— True, sir, you 're a pleasant gentleman, but I suppose you understand our business.

Mirabel. Sir, I may go near to guess at your employments; you, sir, are a lawyer, I presume; you, a physician; you, a scrivener; you, a stockjobber.— *Aside.* All cut-throats, egad!

Fourth Bravo. Sir, I am a broken officer. I was cashiered at the head of the army for a coward: so I took up the trade of murder to retrieve the reputation of my courage.

Third Bravo. I am a soldier too, and would serve my king, but I don't like the quarrel, and I have more honour than to fight in a bad cause.

Second Bravo. I was bred a gentleman, and have no estate, but I must have my . . . . and my bottle, through the prejudice of education.

First Bravo. I am a ruffian too, by the prejudice of education; I was bred a butcher. In short, sir, if your wine had come, we might have trifled a little longer.—Come, sir, which sword will you fall by? mine, sir? *Draws.*

Second Bravo. Or mine? *Draws.*

Third Bravo. Or mine? *Draws.*

Fourth Bravo. Or mine? *Draws.*

Mirabel. Aside. I scorn to beg my life; but to be butchered thus— *Knocking.*

Oh, there's the wine!—This moment for my life or death.

Enter ORIANA.

Lost, for ever lost!—*Faintly.* Where's the wine, child?

Oriana. Coming up, sir. *Stamps.*

Enter Captain DURETETE *with his sword drawn, and six soldiers with their pieces presented; the Bravoes drop their swords. Exit* ORIANA.

Mirabel. The wine! the wine! the wine! Youth, pleasure, fortune, days, and years, are now my own again.—Ah, my dear friends, did not I tell you this wine would make me merry?—Dear captain, these gentlemen are the best-natured, facetious, witty creatures, that ever you knew.

Enter LAMORCE.

Lamorce. Is the wine come, sir?

Mirabel. O yes, madam, the wine is come—see there!— *Pointing to the Soldiers.* Your ladyship has got a very fine ring upon your finger.

Lamorce. Sir, 'tis at your service.

Mirabel. O ho! is it so? *Puts it on his finger.* Thou dear seven hundred pound, thou'rt welcome home again, with all my heart!—Ad's my life, madam, you have got the finest built watch there! Tompion's, I presume?

Lamorce. Sir, you may wear it.

Mirabel. O madam, by no means, 'tis too much!—Rob you of all!— *Taking it from her.* Good dear time, thou 'rt a precious thing: I'm glad I have retrieved thee.— *Putting it up.* What, my friends neglected all this while! Gentlemen, you'll pardon my complaisance to the lady.—How now, is it so civil to be out of humour at my entertainment, and I so pleased with yours?—*To* DURETETE. Captain, you 're surprised at all this! but we 're in our frolics you must know.—Some wine here!

Enter Servant with wine.

Come, captain, this worthy gentleman's health.— *Tweaks First Bravo by the nose; he roars.* But now, where, where's my dear deliverer, my boy, my charming boy?

First Bravo. I hope some of our crew below stairs have despatched him.

Mirabel. Villain, what sayest thou? despatched! I'll have ye all tortured, racked, torn to pieces alive, if you have touched my boy.—Here, page! page! page! *Runs out.*

Duretete. Here, gentlemen, be sure you secure those fellows.

First Bravo. Yes, sir, we know you and your guard will be very civil to us.

Duretete. Take 'em to justice.

Exeunt Soldiers with the Bravoes.

Enter Old MIRABEL *and Others.*

Old Mirabel. Robin ! Robin ! where 's Bob, where 's my boy ? . . .

Re-enter MIRABEL.

Ah, my dear Bob, art thou safe, man?

Mirabel. No, no, sir, I 'm ruined, the saver of my life is lost.

Old Mirabel. No, no, he came and brought us the news.

Mirabel. But where is he?

Re-enter ORIANA.

Ha ! *Runs and embraces her.* My dear preserver, what shall I do to recompense your trust? Father, friend, gentlemen, behold the youth that has relieved me from the most ignominious death, from the scandalous poniards of these bloody ruffians, where to have fallen, would have defamed my memory with vile reproach.—My life, estate, my all, is due to such a favour. Command me, child : before you all, before my late, so kind indulgent stars, I swear, to grant whate'er you ask.

Oriana. To the same stars indulgent now to me, I will appeal as to the justice of my claim ; I shall demand but what was mine before—the just performance of your contract to Oriana. *Discovering herself.*

All. Oriana !

Oriana. In this disguise I resolved to follow you abroad, counterfeited that letter that got me into your service; and so, by this strange turn of fate, I became the instrument of your preservation. Few common servants would have had such cunning: my love inspired me with the meaning of your message, 'cause my concern for your safety made me suspect your company.

THE RECRUITING OFFICER

THE plot of this good broad comedy needs for the understanding of our extract from it no further setting forth than the statement that Captain Plume, an easy-going fine gentleman officer, and Sergeant Kite, a knavish soldier, are engaged on a recruiting expedition to Shrewsbury, and that Costar and Appletree, their dupes, are two countrymen.

The Market-Place. Drum beats the Grenadier's March.

Enter Sergeant KITE, *followed by* THOMAS APPLE-TREE, COSTAR PEARMAIN, *and the Mob.*

Kite. Making a speech. If any gentlemen soldiers, or others, have a mind to serve Her Majesty, and pull down the French king: if any prentices have severe masters, any children have undutiful parents: if any servants have too little wages, or any husband too much wife: let them repair to the noble sergeant Kite, at the sign of the Raven, in this good town of Shrewsbury, and they shall receive present relief and entertainment.

—Gentlemen, I don't beat my drums here to ensnare or inveigle any man; for you must know, gentlemen, that I am a man of honour; besides, I don't beat up for common soldiers; no, I list only grenadiers, grenadiers, gentlemen. Pray, gentlemen, observe this cap. This is the cap of honour, it dubs a man a gentleman in the drawing of a trigger; and he that has the good fortune to be born six foot high, was born to be a great man. *To* COSTAR PEARMAIN. Sir, will you give me leave to try this cap upon your head?

Cos. Is there no harm in 't? Won't the cap list me?

Kite. No, no, no more than I can.—Come, let me see how it becomes you.

Cos. Are you sure there be no conjuration in it? no gunpowder plot upon me?

Kite. No, no, friend; don't fear, man.

Cos. My mind misgives me plaguily. Let me see it.
Going to put it on.
It smells woundily of brimstone. Smell, Tummas.

Tho. Ay, wauns does it.

Cos. Pray, sergeant, what writing is this upon the face of it?

Kite. The crown, or the bed of honour.

Cos. Pray, now, what may be that same bed of honour.

Kite. Oh, a mighty large bed! bigger by half than the great bed at Ware—ten thousand people may lie in it together, and never feel one another.

Cos. My wife and I would do well to lie in 't. But do folk sleep sound in this same bed of honour?

Kite. Sound!—Ay, so sound that they never wake.

Cos. Wauns! I wish again that my wife lay there.

Kite. Say you so? Then I find, brother—

Cos. Brother!—Hold there, friend; I am no kindred to you that I know of yet. Look'e, sergeant, no coaxing—no wheedling, d'ye see: if I have a mind to list, why so; if not, why 'tis not so: therefore, take your cap and your brothership back again, for I an't disposed at this present writing.—No coaxing, no brothering me, faith!

Kite. I coax! I wheedle! I'm above it! Sir, I have served twenty campaigns. But, sir, you talk well, and I must own that you are a man, every inch of you, a pretty young sprightly fellow. I love a fellow with a spirit, but I scorn to coax—'tis base; though I must say, that never in my life have I seen a better built man. How firm and strong he treads!—he steps like a castle! Come, honest lad, will you take share of a pot!

Cos. Nay, for that matter, I'll spend my penny with the best he that wears a head; that is, begging your pardon, sir, and in a fair way.

Kite. Give me your hand, then; and now, gentlemen, I have no more to say but this—here's a purse of gold, and there is a tub of humming ale at my quarters: 'tis the queen's money, and the queen's drink.—She's a generous queen, and loves her subjects.—I hope, gentlemen, you won't refuse the queen's health?

Mob. No, no, no!

Kite. Huzza, then! huzza for the queen, and the honour of Shropshire!

Mob. Huzza!   *Exeunt, shouting, drum beating the 'Grenadier's March.'*

. . . .

Re-enter KITE, *and* PLUME.

Kite. Welcome to Shrewsbury, noble captain! From the banks of the Danube to the Severn side, noble captain, you 're welcome!

Plume. A very elegant reception, indeed, Mr. Kite! I find you are fairly entered into your recruiting strain: pray, what success?

Kite. I 've been here but a week, and I have recruited five.

Plume. Five! Pray what are they?

Kite. I have listed the strong man of Kent, the king of the gipsies, a Scotch pedlar, a scoundrel attorney, and a Welsh parson.

Plume. An attorney! Wert thou mad? List a lawyer! Discharge him, discharge him this minute.

Kite. Why, sir?

Plume. Because I will have nobody in my company that can write; a fellow that can write can draw petitions. I say, this minute discharge him.

Kite. And what shall I do with the parson?
Plume. Can he write?
Kite. Hum! He plays rarely upon the fiddle.
Plume. Keep him, by all means.—But how stands the country affected? Were the people pleased with the news of my coming to town?
Kite. Sir, the mob are so pleased with your honour, and the justices and better sort of people, are so delighted with me, that we shall soon do our business.

The Street.

Enter Sergeant KITE, *leading* COSTAR PEARMAIN *in one hand, and* THOMAS APPLETREE *in the other, both drunk.*

Kite. Sings. *Our 'prentice, Tom, may now refuse*
  To wipe his scoundrel master's shoes;
  For now he's free to sing and play,
  Over the hills and far away.   Over, etc.

Kite. Hey, boys! thus we soldiers live; drink, sing, dance, play! We live, as one should say—we live—'tis impossible to tell how we live. We are all princes. Why, why, you are a king—you are an emperor, and I'm a prince. Now, an't we?
Tho. No, sergeant, I'll be no emperor.
Kite. No!
Tho. I'll be a justice of peace.

o

Kite. A justice of peace, man!

Tho. Ay, wauns will I; for, since this pressing act, they are greater than any emperor under the sun.

Kite. Done! you are a justice of peace, and you are a king, and I am a duke; and a rum duke, an't I?

Cos. Ay, but I'll be no king.

Kite. What then?

Cos. I'll be a queen.

Kite. A queen!

Cos. Ay, Queen of England; that's greater than any king of them all.

Kite. Bravely said, faith! huzza for the queen!
Huzza.

But hark'ee, you Mr. Justice, and you, Mr. Queen, did you ever see the queen's picture?

Both. No! no! no!

Kite. I wonder at that; I have two of them set in gold, and as like Her Majesty, bless the mark!—see here, they are set in gold.

Takes two broad-pieces out of his pocket, and gives one to each.

Tho. The wonderful works of Nature!
Looking at it.

Cos. What's this written about? Here's a posy, I believe.—*Ca-ro-lus!*—What's that, sergeant?

Kite. O! Carolus!—Why, Carolus is Latin for Queen Anne,—that's all.

Cos. 'Tis a fine thing to be a scollard!—Sergeant,

will you part with this? I'll buy it on you, if it come within the compass of a crawn.

Kite. A crown! never talk of buying; 'tis the same thing among friends, you know; I'll present them to ye both: you shall give me as good a thing. Put 'em up, and remember your old friend when I am—*Over the hills and far away. They sing and put up the money.*

Enter Captain PLUME, *singing.*

Plume. *Over the hills and over the main,*
To Flanders, Portugal, or Spain:
The queen commands, and we'll obey,
Over the hills and far away.

Come on, my men of mirth, away with it, I'll make one among ye.—Who are these hearty lads?

Kite. Off with your hats—'ounds! off with your hats! This is the captain, the captain!

Tho. We have seen captains afore now, mun!

Cos. Ay, and lieutenant-captains, too; flesh; I'll keep on my nab.

Tho. And I'se scarcely doff mine for any captain in England. My vether's a freeholder.

Plume. Who are these jolly lads, sergeant?

Kite. A couple of honest brave fellows, that are willing to serve the queen: I have entertained 'em just now as volunteers, under your honour's command.

Plume. And good entertainment they shall have.

Volunteers are the men I want, those are the men fit to make soldiers, captains, generals.

Cos. Wauns, Tummas, what's this! are you listed?

Tho. Flesh! not I: are you, Costar?

Cos. Wauns! not I.

Kite. What! not listed! Ha! ha! ha! a very good jest, i' faith.

Cos. Come, Tummas, we'll go home.

Tho. Ay, ay, come.

Kite. Home! for shame, gentlemen, behave yourselves better before your captain! Dear Tummas, honest Costar!

Tho. No, no! we'll be gone.

Kite. Nay, then, I command you to stay: I place you both sentinels in this place for two hours, to watch the motion of St. Mary's clock you; and you the motion of St. Chad's: and he that dares stir from his post till he be relieved, shall have my sword in him the next minute.

Plume. What's the matter, sergeant? I'm afraid you are too rough with these gentlemen.

Kite. I'm too mild, sir: they disobey command, sir, and one of 'em should be shot for an example to the other.

Cos. Shot, Tummas!

Plume. Come, gentlemen, what's the matter?

Tho. We don't know; the noble sergeant is pleased to be in a passion, sir—but—

Kite. They disobey command; they deny their being listed.

Tho. Nay, sergeant, we don't downright deny it neither; that we dare not do, for fear of being shot: but we humbly conceive in a civil way, and begging your worship's pardon, that we may go home.

Plume. That's easily known. Have either of you received any of the queen's money?

Cos. Not a brass farthing, sir.

Kite. They have each of them received three-and-twenty shillings and sixpence, and 'tis now in their pockets.

Cos. Wauns! if I have a penny in my pocket but a bent sixpence, I'll be content to be listed, and shot into the bargain!

Tho. And I. Look ye here, sir.

Cos. Ay, here's my stock too: nothing but the queen's picture, that the sergeant gave me just now.

Kite. See there, a broad-piece! three-and-twenty shillings and sixpence; t' other has the fellow on 't.

Plume. The case is plain, gentlemen, the goods are found upon you. Those pieces of gold are worth three-and-twenty and sixpence each.

Whispers Sergeant KITE.

Cos. So it seems that *Carolus* is three-and-twenty shillings and sixpence in Latin.

Tho. 'Tis the same thing in Greek, for we are listed.

Cos. Flesh! but we an't, Tummas!—I desire to be carried before the mayor, captain.

Plume. Aside to KITE. 'Twill never do, Kite—your damned tricks will ruin me at last.—I won't lose the fellows, though, if I can help it. *Aloud.* Well, gentlemen, there must be some trick in this; my sergeant offers here to take his oath that you are fairly listed.

Tho. Why, captain, we know that you soldiers have more liberty of conscience than other folks; but for me or neighbour Costar here, to take such an oath, 'twould be downright perjuration.

Plume. Look 'ee you rascal! you villain! If I find that you have imposed upon these two honest fellows, I'll trample you to death, you dog!—Come, how was 't?

Tho. Nay, then, we will speak. Your sergeant, as you say, is a rogue, begging your worship's pardon—and—

Cos. Nay, Tummas, let me speak; you know I can read.—And so, sir, he gave us those two pieces of money for pictures of the queen, by way of a present.

Plume. How! by way of a present! the son of a gun! I'll teach him to abuse honest fellows like you! —Scoundrel, rogue, villain!

                Beats off Sergeant KITE, *and follows.*

Both. O brave noble captain! huzza! A brave captain, 'faith!

Cos. Now, Tummas, *Carolus* is Latin for a beating. This is the bravest captain I ever saw.—Wauns! I have a month's mind to go with him.

Re-enter Captain PLUME.

Plume. A dog, to abuse two such pretty fellows as you.—Look'ee, gentlemen, I love a pretty fellow: I come among you as an officer to list soldiers, not as a kidnapper to steal slaves.

Cos. Mind that, Tummas.

Plume. I desire no man to go with me but as I went myself. I went a volunteer, as you, or you, may do; for a little time carried a musket, and now I command a company.

Tho. Mind that, Costar.—A sweet gentleman!

Plume. 'Tis true, gentlemen, I might take an advantage of you; the queen's money was in your pockets—my sergeant was ready to take his oath you were listed; but I scorn to do a base thing, you are both of you at your liberty.

Cos. Thank you, noble captain.—Ecod! I can't find in my heart to leave him, he talks so finely.

Tho. Ay, Costar, would he always hold in this mind.

Plume. Come, my lads, one thing more I'll tell you: you're both young tight fellows, and the army is the place to make you men for ever: every man has his lot, and you have your's. What think you now of a purse full of French gold out of a monsieur's pocket, after you have dashed out his brains with the but of your firelock, eh?

Cos. Wauns! I'll have it, captain—give me a shilling, I'll follow you to the end of the world.

Tho. Nay, dear Costar! do 'na: be advised.

Plume. Here, my hero, here are two guineas for thee, as earnest of what I'll do farther for thee.

Tho. Do 'na take it; do 'na, dear Costar.

Cries, and pulls back his arm.

Cos. I wull! I wull!—Wauns! my mind gives me, that I shall be a captain myself.—I take your money, sir, and now I am a gentleman.

Plume. Give me thy hand, and now you and I will travel the world o'er, and command it wherever we tread. *Aside to* COSTAR PEARMAIN. Bring your friend with you, if you can. *Aside.*

Cos. Well, Tummus, must we part?

Tho. No, Costar, I canno leave thee.—Come, captain, I'll e'en go along, too; and, if you have two honester, simpler lads in your company, than we twa been, I'll say no more.

Plume. Here, my lad. *Gives him money.* Now, your name?

Tho. Tummas Appletree.

Plume. And yours?

Cos. Costar Pearmain.

Plume. Born where?

Tho. Both in Herefordshire.

Plume. Very well; courage, my lads!—Now we'll sing, ' *Over the hills, and far away.*' *Sings.*

*Courage, boys, 'tis one to ten
But we return all gentlemen;
While conquering colours we display,
Over the hills, and far away.*

Exeunt singing.

JOHN GAY

Born 1688.   Died 1732.

GAY never attempted real comedy as Addison and Steele, his contemporaries, did. They both failed. Gay, who did not presume to call his piece a comedy, yet came very near to writing in the right comedy vein. His celebrated 'Beggar's Opera' was, it is recorded, the expansion into dramatic form of a suggestion of Dean Swift to write a Newgate pastoral. Neither Swift nor his friend and associate Gay were troubled with those moralizing tendencies of the age which may have hindered Addison and Steele in the attainment of comedy—consequently Gay's clear genius for the stage, his wit, and his knowledge of the world, suffered no hindrance when he attempted comedy-writing. The 'Beggar's Opera' is, in fact, rather the parody of a comedy interspersed with songs than a true opera, but there are passages in it which, abating some necessary absurdity, are wholly in the comedy vein. The play is unfortunately too gross for a more liberal extract than has been given. In reading the 'Beggar's Opera,' it is good to remember the wonderful success of the play in its own day. Phrases from it passed as catch-words in society, and its admirable songs were painted on ladies' fans.

JOHN GAY

THE BEGGAR'S OPERA

THE 'Beggar's Opera' begins with a short introductory dialogue between a Player and the Beggar who is the supposed author of the opera.

The plot turns upon the adventures of the gallant and dashing Captain Macheath, the leader of a band of highwaymen who dispose of their booty to two informers and receivers of stolen goods, Peachum and Lockit, the Newgate gaoler. Macheath has privately married Polly, Peachum's daughter, and Lucy Lockit thinks she has equal claims upon him. Polly's parents upbraid her with her marriage, and urge her to betray Macheath into their hands. She refuses, but Peachum soon after succeeds in arresting him through the treachery of some of his gang.

In Newgate, Macheath is visited by the two rivals Polly and Lucy. By stealing her father's keys Lucy contrives his escape, but before long he is once more taken captive, is sentenced to instant execution for breaking prison, and led off by the sheriff's officers.

The Beggar and Player of the Introduction now reappear, and the Player expostulates with the Beggar on the impropriety of so tragic a termination to the opera as the hanging of Captain Macheath. The Beggar, upon this, consents to allow the catastrophe to be averted; Captain Macheath is reprieved, declares his marriage with Polly, and the opera ends with dance and song.

PEACHUM'S *House.*

PEACHUM, Mrs. PEACHUM, *and* POLLY.

Peachum. . . . But now, Polly, to your affair; for matters must not be as they are. You are married then, it seems?

Polly. Yes, Sir.

Peachum. And how do you propose to live, child?

Polly. Like other women, Sir, upon the industry of my husband.

Mrs. Peachum. What, is the wench turn'd fool? A highway-man's wife, like a soldier's, hath as little of his pay as of his company.

Peachum. And had you not the common views of a gentlewoman in your marriage, Polly?

Polly. I don't know what you mean, Sir.

Peachum. Of a jointure, and of being a widow.

Polly. But I love him, Sir: how then could I have thoughts of parting with him?

Peachum. Parting with him! Why, that is the whole scheme and intention of all marriage-articles. The comfortable estate of widowhood is the only hope that keeps up a wife's spirits. Where is the woman who would scruple to be a wife, if she had it in her power to be a widow whenever she pleased? If you have any views of this sort, Polly, I shall think the match not so very unreasonable.

Polly. How I dread to hear your advice! Yet I must beg you to explain yourself.

Peachum. Secure what he hath got, have him peach'd the next sessions, and then at once you are made a rich widow.

Polly. What, murder the man I love! The blood runs cold at my heart with the very thought of it.

Peachum. Fie, Polly! what hath murder to do in the affair? Since the thing sooner or later must happen, I dare say the Captain himself would like that we should get the reward for his death sooner than a stranger. Why, Polly, the Captain knows, that as 'tis his employment to rob, so 'tis ours to take robbers; every man in his business. So that there is no malice in the case.

Mrs. Peachum. Ay, husband, now you have nick'd the matter. To have him peach'd is the only thing could ever make me forgive her.

AIR, 'Now ponder well, ye parents dear.'

Polly. *Oh, ponder well, be not severe;*
So save a wretched wife!
For on the rope that hangs my dear,
Depends poor Polly's life.

Mrs. Peachum. But your duty to your parents, hussy, obliges you to hang him. What would many a wife give for such an opportunity!

Polly. What is a jointure, what is widowhood to me? I know my heart. I cannot survive him.

  AIR, '*Le printemps rappelle aux armes.*'
  The turtle thus with plaintive crying,
   Her lover dying,
  The turtle thus with plaintive crying
   Laments her dove.
  Down she drops quite spent with sighing,
   Pair'd in death, as pair'd in love.

Thus, Sir, it will happen to your poor Polly.

Mrs. Peachum. What, is the fool in love in earnest then? I hate thee for being particular: why, wench, thou art a shame to thy very sex.

Polly. But hear me, mother. . . . If you ever loved—

Mrs. Peachum. Those cursed play-books she reads have been her ruin. One word more, hussy, and I shall knock your brains out, if you have any.

Peachum. Keep out of the way, Polly, for fear of mischief, and consider of what is proposed to you.

Mrs. Peachum. Away, hussy. Hang your husband and be dutiful.   POLLY *listening.*
The thing, husband, must and shall be done. For the sake of intelligence we must take other measures, and have him peach'd the next session without her consent. If she will not know her duty, we know ours.

Peachum. But really, my dear, it grieves one's heart to take off a great man. When I consider his personal bravery, his fine stratagem, how much we have already got by him, and how much more we may get, methinks I can't find in my heart to have an hand in his death. I wish you could have made Polly undertake it.

Mrs. Peachum. But in a case of necessity . . . . our own lives are in danger.

Peachum. Then, indeed, we must comply with the customs of the world, and make gratitude give way to interest—He shall be taken off.

Mrs. Peachum. I'll undertake to manage Polly.

Peachum. And I'll prepare matters for the Old Bailey.   *Exeunt* PEACHUM *and Mrs.* PEACHUM.

Polly. Now, I'm a wretch, indeed. . . . Methinks I see him already in the cart, sweeter and more lovely than the nosegay in his hand!—I hear the crowd extolling his resolution and intrepidity!—What volleys of sighs are sent from the windows of Holborn, that so comely a youth should be brought to disgrace! —I see him at the tree! the whole circle are in tears! —even butchers weep!—Jack Ketch himself hesitates to perform his duty, and would be glad to lose his fee, by a reprieve. What then will become of Polly!—As yet I may inform him of their design, and aid him in his escape.—It shall be so.

Newgate.

MACHEATH, LUCY. *Enter* POLLY.

Polly. Where is my dear husband?—Was a rope ever intended for this neck!—Oh, let me throw my arms about it and throttle thee with love!—Why dost thou turn away from me?—'Tis thy Polly—'tis thy wife.

Macheath. Was ever such an unfortunate rascal as I am!

Lucy. Was there ever such another villain!

Polly. Oh, Macheath! was it for this we parted? Taken! Imprisoned! Tried! Hanged!—cruel reflection! I'll stay with thee till death—no force shall tear thy dear wife from thee now.—What means my love? —Not one kind word! not one kind look! Think what thy Polly suffers to see thee in this condition.

Macheath. Aside. I must disown her. The wench is distracted.

Lucy. Can I have no reparation? Sure men were born to lie, and women to believe them! Oh, villain! villain!

Polly. Am I not thy wife?—Thy neglect of me, thy aversion to me too severely proves it.—Look on me. —Tell me, am I not thy wife?

Lucy. Perfidious wretch!

Polly. Barbarous husband!

Lucy. Had'st thou been hanged five months ago, I had been happy.

Polly. And I too.—If you had been kind to me till death, it would not have vexed me—And that's no very unreasonable request (though from a wife) to a man who hath not above seven or eight days to live.

Lucy. Art thou then married to another? Hast thou two wives, monster?

Macheath. If women's tongues can cease for an answer—hear me.

Lucy. I won't.—Flesh and blood can't bear my usage.

Polly. Shall I not claim my own!—Justice bids me speak.

Macheath. *How happy could I be with either*
 Were t'other dear charmer away!
 But while you thus teaze me together
 To neither a word will I say;
 But tol de rol, etc.

Polly. Sure, my dear, there ought to be some preference shown to a wife! At least she may claim the appearance of it. He must be distracted with his misfortunes, or he could not use me thus.

Lucy. Oh, villain, villain! thou hast deceived me— I could even inform against thee with pleasure. . . .

Macheath. Be pacified, my dear Lucy—This is all a fetch of Polly's to make me desperate with you in case I get off. If I am hanged, she would fain have the credit of being thought my widow—Really, Polly, this is no time for a dispute of this sort; for whenever you are talking of marriage, I am thinking of hanging.

Polly. And hast thou the heart to persist in disowning me?

Macheath. And hast thou the heart to persist in persuading me that I am married? Why, Polly, dost thou seek to aggravate my misfortunes?

Lucy. Really, Miss Peachum, you but expose yourself. Besides, 'tis barbarous in you to worry a gentleman in his circumstances.

Polly. Decency, Madam, methinks, might teach you to behave yourself with some reserve with the husband, while his wife is present.

Macheath. But seriously, Polly, this is carrying the joke a little too far.

Lucy. If you are determined, Madam, to raise a disturbance in the prison, I shall be obliged to send for the turnkey to shew you the door. I am sorry, Madam, you force me to be so ill-bred.

Polly. Give me leave to tell you, Madam; these forward airs don't become you in the least, Madam. And my duty, Madam, obliges me to stay with my husband, Madam.

GOLDSMITH

Born 1728.   Died 1774.

GOLDSMITH, like Sheridan, borrowed a good deal of his comedy manner from the dramatists of the Restoration period. In the making of plays, more perhaps than in any other form of composition, a writer, having to act directly upon the traditional and conventionalized tastes of audiences, cannot safely overlook the work of his predecessors. Goldsmith's immediate predecessors were the playwrights of the sentimental school. His literary taste and keen sense of humour revolted against their general badness and their bathos, and he went back for models to the dramatists of the Restoration,—a term, be it observed, which has much more than a chronological significance,—and both Goldsmith and Sheridan may in a sense be taken to be the last representatives of the great Restoration School of Comedy. He is a more original writer than Sheridan—his plots are mostly his own, and with, I think, two exceptions, his characters are entirely so, but his originality is partly due to this, that he departed at times from the purposes of comedy and got distinctly into the region of farce. Yet this farce element was what, if tradition is true, mainly saved his first piece from damnation; for the first-night's audience, it is recorded, chose to consider 'The Good-Natured Man' not up to their standard of refinement in comedy. They were a little shocked (not wholly without reason) by the impossibility and absurdity of the scene where Honeywood passes off the bailiffs who come to arrest him as gentleman acquaintances, and were cold and critical till Shuter came on in the part of Croaker to read that famous incendiary letter in which Goldsmith's fun is at its best and broadest: this won the audience, and the most humorous comedy in the English language was fortunately saved. 'She Stoops to Conquer,' though the farce element is strong in it, is a truer and better comedy than Goldsmith's first piece, and full of that delicate and delightful manner which makes Goldsmith a writer apart from all others.

GOLDSMITH

THE GOOD-NATURED MAN

MR. HONEYWOOD is a young gentleman whose easy good-nature has involved him in money difficulties, ending in his arrest for debt. Miss Richland, an heiress with whom he is in love, comes, accompanied by Garnet, her maid, to pay him a visit. He induces the bailiff and his follower to feign to be two friends of his, but this does not deceive Miss Richland, who has heard of his situation and already instructed her lawyer to pay his debts.

Miss Richland's guardian, Mr. Croaker, a man of a gloomy and repining temper, wishes his son, Leontine, to marry her. Leontine is in love with Olivia, whose mercenary guardian attempting to force her into a convent in France, she throws herself upon Leontine's protection. He brings her to his family as his sister, who had been brought up from childhood in France, and whom he had been sent to fetch home. Croaker pressing his son's marriage with Miss Richland, Leontine and Olivia elope, accompanied by Jarvis, the old servant of Honeywood, who has promised to supply them with funds; but the bill he gave Leontine is protested, and their flight is delayed. Olivia confesses that she is not Croaker's daughter. Sir William Honeywood (Honeywood's father) knows her to be the child of Sir James Woodville, a former friend of his, and successfully intercedes with Croaker for the young couple; while Honeywood, who declares himself convinced of the dangers of too easy a disposition, comes to an understanding with Miss Richland.

A Room in Young HONEYWOOD'S House.

HONEYWOOD.

Honeywood. There is something in my friend Croaker's conversation that entirely depresses me. His very mirth is quite an antidote to all gaiety, and his appearance has a stronger effect on my spirits than an undertaker's shop.—Mr. Croaker, this is such a satisfaction—

Enter CROAKER.

Croaker. A pleasant morning to Mr. Honeywood, and many of them. How is this! you look most shockingly to-day, my dear friend. I hope this weather does not affect your spirits. To be sure, if this weather continues—I say nothing—But God send we be all better this day three months!

Honeywood. I heartily concur in the wish, though, I own, not in your apprehensions.

Croaker. May be not. Indeed, what signifies what weather we have in a country going to ruin like ours? Taxes rising and trade falling. Money flying out of the kingdom, and Jesuits swarming into it. I know at this time no less than a hundred and twenty-seven Jesuits between Charing Cross and Temple Bar.

Honeywood. The Jesuits will scarce pervert you or me, I should hope.

Croaker. May be not. Indeed, what signifies whom

they pervert in a country that has scarce any religion to lose? I'm only afraid for our wives and daughters.

Honeywood. I have no apprehensions for the ladies, I assure you.

Croaker. May be not. Indeed, what signifies whether they be perverted or no? The women in my time were good for something. I have seen a lady drest from top to toe in her own manufactures formerly. But now-a-days, the devil a thing of their own manufacture's about them, except their faces.

Honeywood. But, however these faults may be practised abroad, you don't find them at home, either with Mrs. Croaker, Olivia, or Miss Richland?

Croaker. The best of them will never be canonised for a saint when she's dead. By the bye, my dear friend, I don't find this match between Miss Richland and my son much relished, either by one side or t' other.

Honeywood. I thought otherwise.

Croaker. Ah, Mr. Honeywood, a little of your fine serious advice to the young lady might go far: I know she has a very exalted opinion of your understanding.

Honeywood. But would not that be usurping an authority that more properly belongs to yourself?

Croaker. My dear friend, you know but little of my authority at home. People think, indeed, because they see me come out in a morning thus, with a pleasant face, and to make my friends merry, that all's well within. But I have cares that would break a heart of stone. My wife has so encroached upon every one of my privileges, that I'm now no more than a mere lodger in my own house.

Honeywood. But a little spirit exerted on your side might perhaps restore your authority.

Croaker. No, though I had the spirit of a lion! I do rouse sometimes. But what then? always haggling and haggling. A man is tired of getting the better before his wife is tired of losing the victory.

Honeywood. It's a melancholy consideration indeed, that our chief comforts often produce our greatest anxieties, and that an increase to our possessions is but an inlet to new disquietudes.

Croaker. Ah, my dear friend, these were the very words of poor Dick Doleful to me not a week before he made away with himself. Indeed, Mr. Honeywood, I never see you but you put me in mind of poor Dick. Ah, there was merit neglected for you! and so true a friend! we loved each other for thirty years, and yet he never asked me to lend him a single farthing.

Honeywood. Pray what could induce him to commit so rash an action at last.

Croaker. I don't know: some people were malicious enough to say it was keeping company with me; because we used to meet now and then and open our hearts to each other. To be sure I loved to hear him

talk, and he loved to hear me talk ; poor dear Dick !
He used to say that Croaker rhymed to joker ; and so
we used to laugh.—Poor Dick ! *Going to cry.*

Honeywood. His fate affects me.

Croaker. Ah, he grew sick of this miserable life,
where we do nothing but eat and grow hungry, dress
and undress, get up and lie down ; while reason, that
should watch like a nurse by our side, falls as fast asleep
as we do.

Honeywood. Very true, sir ; nothing can exceed the
vanity of our existence, but the folly of our pursuits.
We wept when we came into the world, and every
day tells us why.

Croaker. Ah, my dear friend, it is a perfect satisfaction to be miserable with you. My son Leontine
shan't lose the benefit of such fine conversation. I 'll
just step home for him. I am willing to show him so
much seriousness in one scarce older than himself.
And what if I bring my last letter to the Gazetteer on
the increase and progress of earthquakes ? It will
amuse us, I promise you. I there prove how the late
earthquake is coming round to pay us another visit,
from London to Lisbon, from Lisbon to the Canary
Islands, from the Canary Islands to Palmyra, from
Palmyra to Constantinople, and so from Constantinople
back to London again. *Exit.*

Honeywood. Poor Croaker ! his situation deserves
the utmost pity. I shall scarce recover my spirits these

three days. Sure to live upon such terms is worse than death itself!

Young HONEYWOOD'S House.

Bailiff, HONEYWOOD, *Follower.*

Bailiff. Lookye, Sir, I have arrested as good men as you in my time: no disparagement of you neither: men that would go forty guineas on a game of cribbage. I challenge the town to show a man in more genteeler practice than myself.

Honeywood. Without all question, Mr. ——. I forget your name, Sir?

Bailiff. How can you forget what you never knew? he! he! he!

Honeywood. May I beg leave to ask your name?

Bailiff. Yes, you may.

Honeywood. Then, pray, Sir, what is your name?

Bailiff. That I didn't promise to tell you. He! he! he! A joke breaks no bones, as we say among us that practise the law.

Honeywood. You may have reason for keeping it a secret, perhaps?

Bailiff. The law does nothing without reason. I'm ashamed to tell my name to no man, Sir. If you can show cause, as why, upon a special capus, that I should prove my name—But, come, Timothy Twitch is my name. And, now you know my name, what have you to say to that?

Honeywood. Nothing in the world, good Mr. Twitch, but that I have a favour to ask, that's all.

Bailiff. Ay, favours are more easily asked than granted, as we say among us that practise the law. I have taken an oath against granting favours. Would you have me perjure myself?

Honeywood. But my request will come recommended in so strong a manner, as, I believe you'll have no scruple. *Pulling out his purse.* The thing is only this. I believe I shall be able to discharge this trifle in two or three days at farthest; but as I would not have the affair known for the world, I have thoughts of keeping you, and your good friend here, about me, till the debt is discharged; for which I shall be properly grateful.

Bailiff. Oh, that's another maxum, and altogether within my oath. For certain, if an honest man is to get anything by a thing, there's no reason why all things should not be done in civility.

Honeywood. Doubtless, all trades must live, Mr. Twitch; and yours is a necessary one.

Gives him money.

Bailiff. Oh, your honour; I hope your honour takes nothing amiss as I does, as I does nothing but my duty in so doing. I'm sure no one can say I ever give a gentleman, that was a gentleman, ill usage. If I saw that a gentleman was a gentleman, I have taken money not to see him for ten weeks together.

Honeywood. Tenderness is a virtue, Mr. Twitch.

Bailiff. Ay, Sir, it's a perfect treasure. I love to see a gentleman with a tender heart. I don't know, but I think I have a tender heart myself. If all that I have lost by my heart was put together, it would make a—but no matter for that.

Honeywood. Don't account it lost, Mr. Twitch. The ingratitude of the world can never deprive us of the conscious happiness of having acted with humanity ourselves.

Bailiff. Humanity, Sir, is a jewel. It's better than gold. I love humanity. People may say, that we in our way have no humanity; but I'll show you my humanity this moment. There's my follower here, little Flanigan, with a wife and four children, a guinea or two would be more to him, than twice as much to another. Now, as I can't show him any humanity myself, I must beg leave you'll do it for me.

Honeywood. I assure you, Mr. Twitch, yours is a most powerful recommendation.

Giving money to the Follower.

Bailiff. Sir, you're a gentleman. I see you know what to do with your money. But, to business: we are to be with you here as your friends, I suppose. But set in case company comes.—Little Flanigan here, to be sure, has a good face; a very good face; but then, he is a little seedy, as we say among us that practise the law. Not well in clothes. Smoke the pocket-holes.

Honeywood. Well, that shall be remedied without delay.

Enter Servant.

Servant. Sir, Miss Richland is below.

Honeywood. How unlucky! Detain her a moment. We must improve my good friend little Mr. Flanigan's appearance first. Here, let Mr. Flanigan have a suit of my clothes—quick—the brown and silver—Do you hear?

Servant. That your honour gave away to the begging gentleman that makes verses, because it was as good as new.

Honeywood. The white and gold then.

Servant. That, your honour, I made bold to sell, because it was good for nothing.

Honeywood. Well, the first that comes to hand then. The blue and gold then. I believe Mr. Flanigan will look best in blue. *Exit* FLANIGAN.

Bailiff. Rabbit me, but little Flanigan will look well in anything. Ah, if your honour knew that bit of flesh as well as I do, you'd be perfectly in love with him. There's not a prettier scout in the four counties after a shy-cock than he: scents like a hound; sticks like a weazle. He was master of the ceremonies to the black Queen of Morocco when I took him to follow me.

Re-enter FLANIGAN.

Heh, ecod, I think he looks so well, that I don't care if I have a suit from the same place for myself.

Honeywood. Well, well, I hear the lady coming. Dear Mr. Twitch, I beg you'll give your friend directions not to speak. As for yourself, I know you'll say nothing without being directed.

Bailiff. Never you fear me; I'll show the lady that I have something to say for myself as well as another. One man has one way of talking, and another man has another, that's all the difference between them.

Enter MISS RICHLAND *and* GARNET, *her Maid.*

Miss Richland. You'll be surprised, sir, with this visit. But you know I'm yet to thank you for choosing my little library.

Honeywood. Thanks, madam, are unnecessary; as it was I that was obliged by your commands. Chairs here. Two of my very good friends, Mr. Twitch and Mr. Flanigan. Pray, gentlemen, sit without ceremony.

Miss Richland. Aside. Who can these odd-looking men be! I fear it is as I was informed. It must be so.

Bailiff. After a pause. Pretty weather; very pretty weather for the time of the year, Madam.

Follower. Very good circuit weather in the country.

Honeywood. You officers are generally favourites among the ladies. My friends, Madam, have been upon very disagreeable duty, I assure you. The fair should in some manner recompense the toils of the brave.

Miss Richland. Our officers do indeed deserve every favour. The gentlemen are in the marine service, I presume, Sir?

Honeywood. Why, Madam, they do—occasionally serve in the Fleet, Madam. A dangerous service!

Miss Richland. I'm told so. And I own it has often surprised me, that while we have had so many instances of bravery there, we have had so few of wit at home to praise it.

Honeywood. I grant, Madam, that our poets have not written as our soldiers have fought; but they have done all they could, and Hawke or Amherst could do no more.

Miss Richland. I'm quite displeased when I see a fine subject spoiled by a dull writer.

Honeywood. We should not be so severe against dull writers, Madam. It is ten to one but the dullest writer exceeds the most rigid French critic who presumes to despise him.

Follower. Damn the French, the parle vous, and all that belongs to them.

Miss Richland. Sir!

Honeywood. Ha, ha, ha! honest Mr. Flanigan. A

true English officer, Madam; he's not content with beating the French, but he will scold them too.

Miss Richland. Yet, Mr. Honeywood, this does not convince me but that severity in criticism is necessary. It was our first adopting the severity of French taste, that has brought them in turn to taste us.

Bailiff. Taste us! By the Lord, madam, they devour us. Give monseers but a taste, and I'll be damn'd but they come in for a bellyfull.

Miss Richland. Very extraordinary this!

Follower. But very true. What makes the bread rising? the parle vous that devour us. What makes the mutton fivepence a pound? the parle vous that eat it up. What makes the beer threepence-halfpenny a pot?—

Honeywood. Aside. Ah! the vulgar rogues; all will be out. *Aloud.* Right, gentlemen, very right, upon my word, and quite to the purpose. They draw a parallel, Madam, between the mental taste and that of our senses. We are injured as much by the French severity in the one, as by French rapacity in the other. That's their meaning.

Miss Richland. Though I don't see the force of the parallel, yet I'll own, that we should sometimes pardon books, as we do our friends, that have now and then agreeable absurdities to recommend them.

Bailiff. That's all my eye. The king only can pardon, as the law says: for, set in case—

Honeywood. I'm quite of your opinion, Sir. I see the whole drift of your argument. Yes, certainly, our presuming to pardon any work, is arrogating a power that belongs to another. If all have power to condemn, what writer can be free?

Bailiff. By his habus corpus. His habus corpus can set him free at any time : for, set in case—

Honeywood. I'm obliged to you, Sir, for the hint. If, Madam, as my friend observes, our laws are so careful of a gentleman's person, sure we ought to be equally careful of his dearer part, his fame.

Follower. Ay, but if so be a man's nabb'd, you know—

Honeywood. Mr. Flanigan, if you spoke for ever, you could not improve the last observation. For my own part, I think it conclusive.

Bailiff. As for the matter of that, mayhap—

Honeywood. Nay, Sir, give me leave in this instance to be positive. For where is the necessity of censuring works without genius, which must shortly sink of themselves? what is it but aiming an unnecessary blow against a victim already under the hands of justice?

Bailiff. Justice! O, by the elevens, if you talk about justice, I think I am at home there : for, in a course of law—

Honeywood. My dear Mr. Twitch, I discern what you'd be at, perfectly; and I believe the lady must be sensible of the art with which it is introduced. I suppose you perceive the meaning, Madam, of his course of law?

Miss Richland. I protest, Sir, I do not. I perceive only that you answer one gentleman before he has finished, and the other before he has well begun.

Bailiff. Madam, you are a gentlewoman, and I will make the matter out. This here question is about severity, and justice, and pardon, and the like of they. Now, to explain the thing—

Honeywood. Aside. O! curse your explanations.

Enter Servant.

Servant. Mr. Leontine, Sir, below, desires to speak with you upon earnest business.

Honeywood. Aside. That's lucky. *Aloud.* Dear Madam, you'll excuse me and my good friends here, for a few minutes. There are books, Madam, to amuse you. Come, gentlemen, you know I make no ceremony with such friends. After you, Sir. Excuse me. Well, if I must. But I know your natural politeness.

Bailiff. Before and behind, you know.

Follower. Ay, ay, before and behind, before and behind.

Exeunt HONEYWOOD, *Bailiff, and Follower.*

Miss Richland. What can all this mean, Garnet?

Garnet. Mean, Madam! why, what should it mean, but what Mr. Lofty sent you here to see? These people he calls officers, are officers sure enough; sheriff's officers; bailiffs, Madam.

Miss Richland. Ay, it is certainly so. Well, though his perplexities are far from giving me pleasure, yet I own there is something very ridiculous in them, and a just punishment for his dissimulation.

Garnet. And so they are. But I wonder, Madam, that the lawyer you just employed to pay his debts and set him free, has not done it by this time. He ought at least to have been here before now. But lawyers are always more ready to get a man into troubles than out of them.

CROAKER'S *House.*

OLIVIA, GARNET. *Enter* JARVIS.

Olivia. O Jarvis, are you come at last? We have been ready this half hour. Now let's be going. Let us fly!

Jarvis. Ay, to Jericho; for we shall have no going to Scotland this bout, I fancy.

Olivia. How! what's the matter?

Jarvis. Money, money, is the matter, Madam. We have got no money. What the plague do you send me of your fool's errand for? My master's bill upon the city is not worth a rush. Here it is; Mrs. Garnet may pin up her hair with it.

Olivia. Undone! How could Honeywood serve us so! What shall we do? Can't we go without it?

Jarvis. Go to Scotland without money! To Scotland without money! Lord, how some people understand geography! We might as well set sail for Patagonia upon a cork-jacket.

Olivia. Such a disappointment! What a base insincere man was your master, to serve us in this manner! Is this his good-nature?

Jarvis. Nay, don't talk ill of my master, Madam. I won't bear to hear anybody talk ill of him but myself.

Garnet. Bless us! now I think on 't, Madam, you need not be under any uneasiness: I saw Mr. Leontine receive forty guineas from his father just before he set out, and he can't yet have left the inn. A short letter will reach him there.

Olivia. Well remembered, Garnet; I'll write immediately. How's this! Bless me, my hand trembles so, I can't write a word. Do you write, Garnet; and, upon second thought, it will be better from you.

Garnet. Truly, Madam, I write and indite but poorly. I never was cute at my larning. But I'll do what I can to please you. Let me see. All out of my own head, I suppose!

Olivia. Whatever you please.

Garnet. *Writing.* Muster Croaker—Twenty guineas, madam?

Olivia. Ay, twenty will do.

Garnet. At the bar of the Talbot till called for.

Expedition—Will be blown up—All of a flame—Quick despatch—Cupid the little god of love.—I conclude it, Madam, with Cupid: I love to see a love-letter end like poetry.

Olivia. Well, well, what you please, anything. But how shall we send it? I can trust none of the servants of this family.

Garnet. Odso, Madam, Mr. Honeywood's butler is in the next room: he's a dear, sweet man; he'll do anything for me.

Jarvis. He! the dog, he'll certainly commit some blunder. He's drunk and sober ten times a day.

Olivia. No matter. Fly, Garnet; anybody we can trust will do. *Exit* GARNET.
Well, Jarvis, now we can have nothing more to interrupt us; you may take up the things and carry them on to the inn. Have you no hands, Jarvis?

Jarvis. Soft and fair, young lady. You, that are going to be married, think things can never be done too fast; but we, that are old, and know what we are about, must elope methodically, Madam.

Olivia. Well, sure, if my indiscretions were to be done over again—

Jarvis. My life for it, you would do them ten times over.

Olivia. Why will you talk so? If you knew how unhappy they make me—

Jarvis. Very unhappy, no doubt: I was once just

as unhappy when I was going to be married myself. I'll tell you a story about that—

Olivia. A story! when I'm all impatience to be away. Was there ever such a dilatory creature!—

Jarvis. Well, Madam, if we must march, why we will march, that's all. Though, odds-bobs, we have still forgot one thing; we should never travel without —a case of good razors, and a box of shaving powder. But no matter, I believe we shall be pretty well shaved by the way. *Going.*

Enter GARNET.

Garnet. Undone, undone, Madam. Ah, Mr. Jarvis, you said right enough. As sure as death, Mr. Honeywood's rogue of a drunken butler dropped the letter before he went ten yards from the door. There's old Croaker has just picked it up, and is this moment reading it to himself in the hall.

Olivia. Unfortunate! we shall be discovered.

Garnet. No, Madam; don't be uneasy; he can neither make head nor tail of it. To be sure he looks as if he was broke loose from Bedlam about it, but he can't find what it means, for all that. O lud, he is coming this way all in the horrors.

Olivia. Then let us leave the house this instant, for fear he should ask further questions. In the mean time, Garnet, do you write and send off just such another. *Exeunt.*

Enter CROAKER.

Croaker. Death and destruction! Are all the horrors of air, fire and water, to be levelled only at me? Am I only to be singled out for gunpowder-plots, combustibles, and conflagration! Here it is—an incendiary letter dropped at my door. 'To Muster Croaker, these with speed.' Ay, ay, plain enough the direction: all in the genuine incendiary spelling, and as cramp as the devil. 'With speed.' O confound your speed. But let me read it once more. *Reads.* 'Muster Croaker, as sone as yow see this, leve twenty gunnes at the bar of the Talboot tell caled for, or yowe and yower experetion wil be al blown up.' Ah, but too plain. Blood and gunpowder in every line of it. Blown up! murderous dog! all blown up! Heavens! what have I and my poor family done, to be all blown up? *Reads.* 'Our pockets are low, and money we must have.' Ay, there's the reason; they'll blow us up, because they have got low pockets. *Reads.* 'It is but a short time you have to consider; for if this takes wind, the house will quickly be all of a flame.' Inhuman monsters! blow us up, and then burn us! The earthquake at Lisbon was but a bonfire to it. *Reads.* 'Make quick despatch, and so no more at present. But may Cupid, the little god of love, go with you wherever you go.' The little god of love! Cupid, the little god of love, go with me! Go you to the devil, you and your little Cupid together. I'm so frightened I scarce know whether I sit, stand, or go. Perhaps this moment I'm treading on lighted matches, blazing brimstone, and barrels of gunpowder. They are preparing to blow me up into the clouds. Murder! we shall be all burnt in our beds; we shall be all burnt in our beds.

Enter Miss RICHLAND.

Miss Richland. Lord, Sir, what's the matter.

Croaker. Murder's the matter. We shall all be blown up in our beds before morning.

Miss Richland. I hope not, Sir.

Croaker. What signifies what you hope, Madam, when I have a certificate of it here in my hand? Will nothing alarm my family? Sleeping and eating, sleeping and eating, is the only work from morning till night in my house. My insensible crew could sleep though rocked by an earthquake, and fry beefsteaks at a volcano.

Miss Richland. But, Sir, you have alarmed them so often already; we have nothing but earthquakes, famines, plagues, and mad dogs, from year's end to year's end. You remember, Sir, it is not above a month ago, you assured us of a conspiracy among the bakers, to poison us in our bread; and so kept the whole family a week upon potatoes.

Croaker. And potatoes were too good for them.

But why do I stand talking here with a girl, when I should be facing the enemy without? Here, John, Nicodemus, search the house. Look into the cellars, to see if there be any combustibles below; and above, in the apartments, that no matches be thrown in at the windows. Let all the fires be put out, and let the engine be drawn out in the yard, to play upon the house in case of necessity. *Exit.*

SHE STOOPS TO CONQUER

Two young men, Marlow and Hastings, are on their road to the house of Mr. Hardcastle, an old-fashioned country gentleman, whose family consists of his wife and daughter, Tony Lumpkin, Mrs. Hardcastle's son by a first marriage, a country bumpkin with low tastes, and Constance Neville, her niece and ward, whom she designs to marry to Tony. Hastings is attached to Miss Neville, and Marlow makes this visit in obedience to his father's wish that he should pay his addresses to Miss Hardcastle, the daughter of his old friend. They are both strangers to all the family, except Miss Neville.

They lose their way, and inquiring at a village alehouse, are directed by Tony Lumpkin to his stepfather's house as the nearest inn. Their behaviour consequently astonishes and offends Mr. Hardcastle. Constance presently undeceives Hastings, but they resolve to let Marlow remain in his error, lest he should leave the house at once without seeing Miss Hardcastle. Marlow is invincibly shy in the presence of ladies, and when Miss Hardcastle comes in from walking (he is told that she and Miss Neville have just arrived at the inn), he is constrained and bashful to excess; but when soon after, failing to recognize her in a plain morning dress, he takes her for the barmaid, and after being informed that he is in Mr. Hardcastle's house, for a poor relation of the family, he first admires and then falls in love with her.

Finally his father, Sir Charles Marlow, arrives, all misunderstandings are cleared up;—Hastings marries Constance Neville, and Mr. Hardcastle joins the hands of Marlow and his daughter.

An Alehouse Room.

TONY LUMPKIN. *Enter Landlord.*

Landlord. There be two gentlemen in a post-chaise at the door. They have lost their way upo' the forest; and they are talking something about Mr. Hardcastle.

Tony. As sure as can be, one of them must be the gentleman that's coming down to court my sister. Do they seem to be Londoners?

Landlord. I believe they may They look woundily like Frenchmen.

Tony. Then desire them to step this way, and I'll set them right in a twinkling. *Exit Landlord.* Father-in-law has been calling me whelp and hound this half-year. Now if I pleased I could be so revenged upon the old grumbletonian. But then I'm afraid—afraid of what? I shall soon be worth fifteen hundred a year, and let him frighten me out of *that* if he can.

Enter Landlord, conducting MARLOW *and* HASTINGS.

Marlow. What a tedious uncomfortable day we have had of it! We were told it was but forty miles across the country, and we have come above threescore.

Hastings. And all, Marlow, from that unaccountable reserve of yours, that would not let us inquire more frequently, on the way.

Marlow. I own, Hastings, I am unwilling to lay myself under an obligation to every one I meet, and often stand the chance of an unmannerly answer.

Hastings. At present, however, we are not likely to receive any answer.

Tony. No offence, gentlemen. But I'm told you have been inquiring for one Mr. Hardcastle in these parts. Do you know what part of the country you are in?

Hastings. Not the least, sir, but should thank you for information.

Tony. Nor the way you came?

Hastings. No, sir; but if you can inform us—

Tony. Why, gentlemen, if you know neither the road you are going, nor where you are, nor the road you came, the first thing I have to inform you is, that —you have lost your way.

Marlow. We wanted no ghost to tell us that.

Tony. Pray, gentlemen, may I be so bold as to ask the place from whence you came?

Marlow. That's not necessary towards directing us where we are to go.

Tony. No offence; but question for question is all fair, you know.—Pray, gentlemen, is not this same Hardcastle a cross-grained, old-fashioned, whimsical fellow, with an ugly face, a daughter, and a pretty son?

Hastings. We have not seen the gentleman; but he has the family you mention.

Tony. The daughter, a tall, trapesing, trolloping, talkative maypole—the son, a pretty, well-bred, agreeable youth, that everybody is fond of?

Marlow. Our information differs in this. The daughter is said to be well-bred and beautiful; the son an awkward booby, reared up and spoiled at his mother's apron-string.

Tony. He—he—hem!—Then, gentlemen, all I have to tell you is, that you won't reach Mr. Hardcastle's house this night, I believe.

Hastings. Unfortunate!

Tony. It's a damn'd long, dark, boggy, dirty, dangerous way. Stingo, tell the gentlemen the way to Mr. Hardcastle's— *Winking upon the Landlord.* Mr. Hardcastle's of Quagmire Marsh, you understand me.

Landlord. Master Hardcastle's! Lock-a-daisy, my masters, you're come a deadly deal wrong! When you came to the bottom of the hill, you should have crossed down Squash Lane.

Marlow. Cross down Squash Lane!

Landlord. Then you were to keep straight forward, till you came to four roads.

Marlow. Come to where four roads meet?

Tony. Ay; but you must be sure to take only one of them.

Marlow. O, sir, you're facetious.

Tony. Then keeping to the right, you are to go sideways, till you come upon Crackskull Common: there you must look sharp for the track of the wheel, and go forward till you come to farmer Murrain's barn. Coming to the farmer's barn, you are to turn to the right, and then to the left, and then to the right about again, till you find the old mill—

Marlow. Zounds, man! we could as soon find out the longitude!

Hastings. What's to be done, Marlow?

Marlow. This house promises but a poor reception; though perhaps the landlord can accommodate us.

Landlord. Alack, master, we have but one spare bed in the whole house.

Tony. And to my knowledge that's taken up by three lodgers already. *After a pause, in which the rest seem disconcerted.* I have hit it. Don't you think, Stingo, our landlady could accommodate the gentlemen by the fire-side, with—three chairs and a bolster?

Hastings. I hate sleeping by the fire-side.

Marlow. And I detest your three chairs and a bolster.

Tony. You do, do you?—Then, let me see—what if you go on a mile further to the Buck's Head; the old Buck's Head on the hill, one of the best inns in the whole county?

Hastings. O ho! So we have escaped an adventure for this night, however.

Landlord. Apart to Tony. Sure, you ben't sending them to your father's as an inn, be you?

Tony. Mum, you fool you. Let *them* find that out. *To them.* You have only to keep on straight forward, till you come to a large old house by the road side. You'll see a pair of large horns over the door. That's the sign. Drive up the yard, and call stoutly about you.

Hastings. Sir, we are obliged to you. The servants can't miss the way?

Tony. No, no: but I tell you, though, the landlord is rich, and going to leave off business; so he wants to be thought a gentleman, saving your presence, he! he! he! He'll be for giving you his company; and, ecod, if you mind him, he'll persuade you that his mother was an alderman, and his aunt a justice of peace.

Landlord. A troublesome old blade, to be sure; but a keeps as good wines and beds as any in the whole country.

Marlow. Well, if he supplies us with these, we shall want no further connection. We are to turn to the right, did you say?

Tony. No, no; straight forward. I'll just step myself and show you a piece of the way. *To the Landlord.* Mum!

Landlord. Ah, bless your heart for a sweet, pleasant—damned mischievous son of . . . . *Exeunt.*

An Old-fashioned House.
Enter HARDCASTLE, *followed by three or four awkward Servants.*

Hardcastle. Well, I hope you are perfect in the table exercise I have been teaching you these three days. You all know your posts and your places, and can show that you have been used to good company, without ever stirring from home.

Omnes. Ay, ay.

Hardcastle. When company comes you are not to pop out and stare, and then run in again, like frighted rabbits in a warren.

Omnes. No, no.

Hardcastle. You, Diggory, whom I have taken from the barn, are to make a show at the side-table; and you, Roger, whom I have advanced from the plough, are to place yourself behind my chair. But you're not to stand so, with your hands in your pockets. Take your hands from your pockets, Roger; and from your head, you blockhead you. See how Diggory carries his hands. They're a little too stiff indeed, but that's no great matter.

Diggory. Ay, mind how I hold them. I learned to hold my hands this way when I was upon drill for the militia. And so being upon drill—

Hardcastle. You must not be so talkative, Diggory. You must be all attention to the guests. You must hear us talk, and not think of talking; you must see us drink, and not think of drinking; you must see us eat, and not think of eating.

Diggory. By the laws, your worship, that's parfectly unpossible. Whenever Diggory sees yeating going forward, ecod, he's always wishing for a mouthful himself.

Hardcastle. Blockhead! Is not a belly-full in the kitchen as good as a belly-full in the parlour? Stay your stomach with that reflection.

Diggory. Ecod, I thank your worship, I'll make a shift to stay my stomach with a slice of cold beef in the pantry.

Hardcastle. Diggory, you are too talkative.—Then, if I happen to say a good thing, or tell a good story, at table, you must not all burst out a-laughing, as if you made part of the company.

Diggory. Then, ecod, your worship must not tell the story of Ould Grouse in the gun-room: I can't help laughing at that—he! he! he!—for the soul of me. We have laughed at that these twenty years—ha! ha! ha!

Hardcastle. Ha! ha! ha! The story is a good one. Well, honest Diggory, you may laugh at that—but still remember to be attentive. Suppose one of the company should call for a glass of wine, how will you behave? A glass of wine, Sir, if you please. *To* DIGGORY. Eh, why don't you move?

Diggory. Ecod, your worship, I never have courage till I see the eatables and drinkables brought upo' the table, and then I'm as bauld as a lion.

Hardcastle. What, will nobody move?

First Servant. I'm not to leave this pleace.

Second Servant. I'm sure it's no pleace of mine.

Third Servant. Nor mine, for sartain.

Diggory. Wauns, and I'm sure it canna be mine.

Hardcastle. You numskulls! and so while, like your betters, you are quarrelling for places, the guests must be starved. O you dunces! I find I must begin all over again—But don't I hear a coach drive into the yard? To your posts, you blockheads. I'll go in the mean time and give my old friend's son a hearty reception at the gate. *Exit* HARDCASTLE.

Diggory. By the elevens, my pleace is gone quite out of my head.

Roger. I know that my pleace is to be everywhere.

First Servant. Where the devil is mine?

Second Servant. My pleace is to be no-where at all; and so I 'ze go about my business.

Exeunt Servants, running about as if frighted, different ways.

MARLOW, HASTINGS. *Enter* HARDCASTLE.

Hardcastle. Gentlemen, once more you are heartily welcome. Which is Mr. Marlow? Sir, you are heartily welcome. It 's not my way, you see, to receive my friends with my back to the fire. I like to give them a hearty reception in the old style at my gate. I like to see their horses and trunks taken care of.

Marlow. Aside. He has got our names from the servants already. *To him.* We approve your caution and hospitality, Sir. *To* HASTINGS. I have been thinking, George, of changing our travelling dresses in the morning. I am grown confoundedly ashamed of mine.

Hardcastle. I beg, Mr. Marlow, you 'll use no ceremony in this house.

Hastings. I fancy, Charles, you 're right: the first blow is half the battle. I intend opening the campaign with the white and gold.

Hardcastle. Mr. Marlow—Mr. Hastings—gentlemen—pray be under no constraint in this house. This is Liberty-hall, gentlemen. You may do just as you please here.

Marlow. Yet, George, if we open the campaign too

fiercely at first, we may want ammunition before it is over. I think to reserve the embroidery to secure a retreat.

Hardcastle. Your talking of a retreat, Mr. Marlow, puts me in mind of the Duke of Marlborough, when we went to besiege Denain. He first summoned the garrison—

Marlow. Don't you think the *ventre d'or* waistcoat will do with the plain brown.

Hardcastle. He first summoned the garrison, which might consist of about five thousand men—

Hastings. I think not: brown and yellow mix but very poorly.

Hardcastle. I say, gentlemen, as I was telling you, he summoned the garrison, which might consist of about five thousand men—

Marlow. The girls like finery.

Hardcastle. Which might consist of about five thousand men, well appointed with stores, ammunition, and other implements of war. Now, says the Duke of Marlborough to George Brooks, that stood next to him—You must have heard of George Brooks—I'll pawn my dukedom, says he, but I take that garrison without spilling a drop of blood. So—

Marlow. What, my good friend, if you gave us a glass of punch in the meantime; it would help us to carry on the siege with vigour.

Hardcastle. Punch, Sir! *Aside.* This is the most unaccountable kind of modesty I ever met with.

Marlow. Yes, Sir, punch. A glass of warm punch after our journey, will be comfortable. This is Liberty-hall, you know.

Hardcastle. Here's a cup, Sir.

Marlow. Aside. So this fellow, in his Liberty-hall, will only let us have just what he pleases.

Hardcastle. Taking the cup. I hope you'll find it to your mind. I have prepared it with my own hands, and I believe you'll own the ingredients are tolerable. Will you be so good as to pledge me, Sir? Here, Mr. Marlow, here is to our better acquaintance. *Drinks.*

Marlow. Aside. A very impudent fellow this! but he's a character, and I'll humour him a little. Sir, my service to you. *Drinks.*

Hastings. Aside. I see this fellow wants to give us his company, and forgets that he's an innkeeper before he has learned to be a gentleman.

Marlow. From the excellence of your cup, my old friend, I suppose you have a good deal of business in this part of the country. Warm work, now and then, at elections, I suppose.

Hardcastle. No, Sir, I have long given that work over. Since our betters have hit upon the expedient of electing each other, there is no business 'for us that sell ale.'

Hastings. So then, you have no turn for politics, I find.

Hardcastle. Not in the least. There was a time,

indeed, I fretted myself about the mistakes of government, like other people; but finding myself every day grow more angry, and the government growing no better, I left it to mend itself. Since that, I no more trouble my head about Hyder Ally, or Ally Cawn, than about Ally Croker. Sir, my service to you.

Hastings. So that with eating above stairs, and drinking below, with receiving your friends within, and amusing them without, you lead a good pleasant bustling life of it.

Hardcastle. I do stir about a great deal, that's certain. Half the differences of the parish are adjusted in this very parlour.

Marlow. After drinking. And you have an argument in your cup, old gentleman, better than any in Westminster-hall.

Hardcastle. Ay, young gentleman, that, and a little philosophy.

Marlow. Aside. Well, this is the first time I ever heard of an innkeeper's philosophy.

Hastings. So then, like an experienced general, you attack them on every quarter. If you find their reason manageable, you attack it with your philosophy; if you find they have no reason, you attack them with this. Here's your health, my philosopher. *Drinks.*

Hardcastle. Good, very good, thank you; ha! ha! ha! Your generalship puts me in mind of Prince

Eugene, when he fought the Turks at the battle of Belgrade. You shall hear.

Marlow. Instead of the battle of Belgrade, I believe it's almost time to talk about supper. What has your philosophy got in the house for supper?

Hardcastle. For supper, Sir? *Aside.* Was ever such a request to a man in his own house?

Marlow. Yes, Sir, supper, Sir; I begin to feel an appetite. I shall make devilish work to-night in the larder, I promise you.

Hardcastle. Aside. Such a brazen dog sure never my eyes beheld. *To him.* Why, really, Sir, as for supper, I can't well tell. My Dorothy and the cook-maid settle these things between them. I leave these kind of things entirely to them.

Marlow. You do, do you?

Hardcastle. Entirely. By the by, I believe they are in actual consultation upon what's for supper this moment in the kitchen.

Marlow. Then I beg they'll admit me as one of their privy-council. It's a way I've got. When I travel I always choose to regulate my own supper. Let the cook be called. No offence I hope, Sir?

Hardcastle. O no, Sir, none in the least; yet I don't know how; our Bridget, the cook-maid, is not very communicative upon these occasions. Should we send for her, she might scold us all out of the house.

Hastings. Let's see your list of the larder then. I ask it as a favour. I always match my appetite to my bill of fare.

Marlow. To HARDCASTLE, *who looks at them with surprise.* Sir, he's very right, and it's my way too.

Hardcastle. Sir, you have a right to command here. Here, Roger, bring us the bill of fare for to-night's supper: I believe it's drawn out.—Your manner, Mr. Hastings, puts me in mind of my uncle, Colonel Wallop. It was a saying of his, that no man was sure of his supper till he had eaten it.

Hastings. Aside. All upon the high ropes! His uncle a colonel! we shall soon hear of his mother being a justice of the peace. But let's hear the bill of fare.

Marlow. Perusing. What's here? For the first course; for the second course; for the dessert. The devil, Sir, do you think we have brought down the whole Joiners' Company, or the corporation of Bedford, to eat up such a supper? Two or three little things, clean and comfortable, will do.

Hastings. But let's hear it.

Marlow. Reading. For the first course at the top, a pig, and prune sauce.

Hastings. Damn your pig, I say.

Marlow. And damn your prune sauce, say I.

Hardcastle. And yet, gentlemen, to men that are hungry, pig with prune sauce is very good eating.

Marlow. At the bottom, a calf's tongue and brains.

Hastings. Let your brains be knocked out, my good Sir, I don't like them.

Marlow. Or you may clap them on a plate by themselves. I do.

Hardcastle. Aside. Their impudence confounds me. *To them.* Gentlemen, you are my guests, make what alterations you please. Is there anything else you wish to retrench or alter, gentlemen?

Marlow. Item. A pork pie, a boiled rabbit and sausages, a Florentine, a shaking pudding, and a dish of tiff—taff—taffety cream.

Hastings. Confound your made dishes; I shall be as much at a loss in this house as at a green and yellow dinner at the French Ambassador's table. I'm for plain eating.

Hardcastle. I'm sorry, gentlemen, that I have nothing you like, but if there be anything you have a particular fancy to—

Marlow. Why, really, Sir, your bill of fare is so exquisite that any one part of it is full as good as another. Send us what you please. So much for supper. And now to see that our beds are aired, and properly taken care of.

Hardcastle. I entreat you'll leave all that to me. You shall not stir a step.

Marlow. Leave that to you! I protest, Sir, you

must excuse me, I always look to these things myself.

Hardcastle. I must insist, Sir, you'll make yourself easy on that head.

Marlow. You see I'm resolved on it. *Aside.* A very troublesome fellow this, as I ever met with.

Hardcastle. Well, Sir, I'm resolved at least to attend you. *Aside.* This may be modern modesty, but I never saw anything look so like old-fashioned impudence. *Exeunt MARLOW and HARDCASTLE.*

Mrs. HARDCASTLE, *Miss* NEVILLE, HASTINGS, TONY LUMPKIN.

Tony. . . . Ecod! I tell you, I'll not be made a fool of no longer.

Mrs. Hardcastle. Wasn't it all for your good, viper? Wasn't it all for your good?

Tony. I wish you'd let me and my good alone, then. Snubbing this way when I'm in spirits. If I'm to have any good, let it come of itself; not keep dinging it, dinging it into one so.

Mrs. Hardcastle. That's false; I never see you when you're in spirits. No, Tony, you then go to the alehouse or kennel. I'm never to be delighted with your agreeable wild notes, unfeeling monster!

Tony. Ecod! mamma, your own notes are the wildest of the two.

Mrs. Hardcastle. Was ever the like? But I see he wants to break my heart; I see he does.

Hastings. Dear madam, permit me to lecture the young gentleman a little. I'm certain I can persuade him to his duty.

Mrs. Hardcastle. Well, I must retire. Come, Constance, my love. You see, Mr. Hastings, the wretchedness of my situation : was ever poor woman so plagued with a dear, sweet, pretty, provoking, undutiful boy? *Exeunt Mrs.* HARDCASTLE *and Miss* NEVILLE.

Tony. Singing. *There was a young man riding by,*
  And fain would have his will.
    Rang do didlo dee.

Don't mind her. Let her cry. It's the comfort of her heart. I have seen her and sister cry over a book for an hour together; and they said they liked the book the better the more it made them cry.

Hastings. Then you're no friend to the ladies, I find, my pretty young gentleman?

Tony. That's as I find 'um.

Hastings. Not to her of your mother's choosing, I dare answer? And yet she appears to me a pretty, well-tempered girl.

Tony. That's because you don't know her as well as I. Ecod! I know every inch about her; and there's not a more bitter, cantankerous toad in all Christendom.

Hastings. Aside. Pretty encouragement this for a lover!

Tony. I have seen her since the height of that. She has as many tricks as a hare in a thicket, or a colt the first day's breaking.

Hastings. To me she appears sensible and silent.

Tony. Ay, before company. But when she's with her playmate, she's as loud as a hog in a gate.

Hastings. But there is a meek modesty about her that charms me.

Tony. Yes, but curb her never so little, she kicks up and you're flung in a ditch.

Hastings. Well, but you must allow her a little beauty.—Yes, you must allow her some beauty.

Tony. Bandbox! She's all a made-up thing, mun. Ah! could you but see Bet Bouncer of these parts, you might then talk of beauty. Ecod, she has two eyes as black as sloes, and cheeks as broad and red as a pulpit cushion. She'd make two of she.

Hastings. Well, what say you to a friend that would take this bitter bargain off your hands?

Tony. Anon.

Hastings. Would you thank him that would take Miss Neville, and leave you to happiness and your dear Betsy?

Tony. Ay; but where is there such a friend, for who would take *her?*

Hastings. I am he. If you but assist me, I'll engage to whip her off to France, and you shall never hear more of her.

Tony. Assist you! Ecod I will, to the last drop of my blood. I'll clap a pair of horses to your chaise that shall trundle you off in a twinkling, and may be get you a part of her fortin beside, in jewels, that you little dream of.

Hastings. My dear 'squire, this looks like a lad of spirit.

Tony. Come along, then, and you shall see more of my spirit before you have done with me.   *Singing.*

> *We are the boys*
> *That fears no noise*
> *Where the thundering cannons roar.*
>
>   *Exeunt.*

CUMBERLAND

Born 1732. Died 1811.

There were few departments of literature in which this worthy writer did not do fair journeyman's work, and amid other work he employed himself as a writer of comedies. He who shoots often must hit sometimes. The 'West Indian' has merit in it ; but his characters are all endowed with a superhuman morality.

CUMBERLAND understood stage effect,—particularly of the emotional kind. But he was over-emotional. Modern French playwrights have been reproached for their habit of dragging in '*ma mère*' when they are at a loss for an emotion. Cumberland's chief stage artifice is also after this kind: almost every one of his plays is concerned with the reunion of long-separated or long-lost parents and children. Cumberland seems to have been a vain and rather absurd personage—perhaps from that pedantry and priggishness which is very perceptible in his plays. Goldsmith's good-nature flatters him when he calls him in 'Retaliation,'

'The Terence of England, the mender of hearts ;'

but he laughs a little at his way of bringing none but faultless characters on his stage—

'And Comedy wonders at being so fine;
Like a Tragedy Queen he has dizened her out,
Or rather like Tragedy giving a rout.'

CUMBERLAND

THE WEST INDIAN

THE reader need be informed no further of the plot of this pedantic play, than that the West Indian, Mr. Belcour, a rich young gentleman from the West Indies has arrived by water in London and meets Mr. Stockwell, the merchant and man of business with whom his business has been chiefly transacted. Mr. Stockwell, through a most improbable concurrence of circumstances, happens to be the legitimate father of Mr. Belcour, though the young gentleman is ignorant of the fact. The scene sets forth the first meeting of father and son.

A Drawing-room. Mr. STOCKWELL *discovered.*

Enter Servant.

Serv. Sir, the foreign gentleman is come.

Enter BELCOUR.

Stock. Mr. Belcour, I am rejoiced to see you; you are welcome to England!

Bel. I thank you heartily, good Mr. Stockwell. You and I have long conversed at a distance; now we are met; and the pleasure this meeting gives me amply compensates for the perils I have run through in accomplishing it.

Stock. What perils, Mr. Belcour? I could not have thought you would have made a bad passage at this time o' year.

Bel. Nor did we: courier-like, we came posting to your shores upon the pinions of the swiftest gales that ever blew; 'tis upon English ground all my difficulties have arisen; 'tis the passage from the river-side I complain of.

Stock. Ay, indeed! What obstructions can you have met between this and the river-side?

Bel. Innumerable! Your town is as full of defiles as the island of Corsica; and, I believe, they are as obstinately defended: so much hurry, bustle, and confusion on your quays; so many sugar-casks, porter-buts, and common-councilmen in your streets, that unless a man marched with artillery in his front, 'tis more than the labour of Hercules can effect to make any tolerable way through your town.

Stock. I am sorry you have been so incommoded.

Bel. Why, 'faith, 'twas all my own fault. Accustomed to a land of slaves, and out of patience with the whole tribe of custom-house extortioners, boat-men, tide-waiters, and water-bailiffs, that beset me on all sides, worse than a swarm of musquitoes, I proceeded a little too roughly to brush them away with my rattan. The sturdy rogues took this in dudgeon, and beginning to rebel, the mob chose different sides, and a furious scuffle ensued; in the course of which, my person and apparel suffered so much, that I was obliged to step into the first tavern to refit, before I could make my approaches in any decent trim.

Stock. Aside. All without is as I wish : dear Nature, add the rest, and I am happy. Well, Mr. Belcour, 'tis a rough sample you have had of my countrymen's spirit; but, I trust, you'll not think the worse of them for it.

Bel. Not at all, not at all; I like them the better. Were I only a visitor, I might, perhaps, wish them a little more tractable; but, as a fellow-subject, and a sharer in their freedom, I applaud their spirit, though I feel the effects of it in every bone of my skin.

Stock. Aside. That's well; I like that well. How gladly I could fall upon his neck, and own myself his father!

Bel. Well, Mr. Stockwell, for the first time in my life, here am I in England; at the fountain head of pleasure, in the land of beauty, of arts, and elegancies. My happy stars have given me a good estate, and the conspiring winds have blown me hither to spend it.

Stock. To use it, not to waste it, I should hope; to treat it, Mr. Belcour, not as a vassal, over whom you have a wanton and despotic power, but as a subject, which you are bound to govern with a temperate and restrained authority.

Bel. True, sir, most truly said; mine's a commission, not a right; I am the offspring of distress, and every child of sorrow is my brother: while I have hands to hold, therefore, I will hold them open to mankind. But, sir, my passions are my masters; they take me where they will; and oftentimes they leave to reason and to virtue nothing but my wishes and my sighs.

Stock. Come, come, the man who can accuse, corrects himself.

Bel. Ah! that's an office I am weary of; I wish a friend would take it up. I would to heaven you had leisure for the employ! but did you drive a trade to the four corners of the world, you would not find the task so toilsome as to keep me free from faults.

Stock. Well, I am not discouraged: this candour tells me I should not have the fault of self-conceit to combat; that, at least, is not amongst the number.

Bel. No; if I knew that man on earth who thought more humbly of me than I do of myself, I would take up his opinion, and forego my own.

Stock. And were I to choose a pupil, it should be one of your complexion; so if you'll come along with me, we'll agree upon your admission, and enter on a a course of lectures directly.

Bel. With all my heart. *Exeunt.*

SHERIDAN

Born 1752.   Died 1816.

The inquiring critic who is also an admirer of SHERIDAN's great genius for the stage is apt to be startled and disappointed by finding how much he is indebted to his predecessors, both French and English : whole scenes reveal themselves as being loans from Molière and Wycherley, and some of his best characters have been transferred from so poor a writer as Murphy, Sir Fretful Plagiary and Joseph Surface being the absolute property of this dramatist.

'A curious thing,' says Théophile Gautier, 'and one which day by day is getting to be more certainly proved, is this : that the men of the very highest genius have seldom invented any thing at all, the plots they have worked upon and the nuclei of their compositions have come to them from authors often of the second rank, of men sometimes obscure, sometimes even contemptible. What then differentiates the genius from the hack writer?—simply style and manner: these after all are what constitute the great artist. Any one can chance upon a telling incident, to any one may occur a poetical idea—the art lies in the setting forth, so that others may find the incident telling, or see the poetry of the idea.'

This, of course, is pushing the advocacy of plagiarism and style a little far, and is the pleading of one who was himself an enthusiastic stylist and somewhat lacked of fertility. The argument, however, is peculiarly applicable to Sheridan, whose dramatic genius it is difficult to appraise too highly. Compared even with Congreve himself, he stands high as a dialoguist, for though his wit is not quite so keen or so nimble, or his style quite so polished, his epigrams and jests seem to grow more naturally and unforcedly out of the circumstances of the play ; his geniality, too, is much greater, and is contagious. After a play of Sheridan's we feel on better terms with human nature. His plots are admirable— not solutions of any of the problems of social life as, according to some critics, comedies should be, but easy, pleasant, and fluent, and full, as such ease and pleasantness implies, of much concealed art. The spirit of Sheridan's plays is so thoroughly modern, they are salted with so good and true a wit, have so much of honest stage-craft in them, and are so full of a humour which is wholly that of the present period, that a play of his adequately put upon the stage will hold its own to this day triumphantly against the most successful of modern pieces.

SHERIDAN

THE SCHOOL FOR SCANDAL

CHARLES SURFACE, an extravagant young gentleman of the town, has run through his fortune. In his extremity, Moses, a Jew usurer, is applied to. Sir Oliver Surface, Charles's uncle, a rich Indian nabob, has, unknown to his nephews Charles and Joseph, returned to England, and visits both nephews in disguise. He applies to Joseph in the character of a poor relation, and is repelled civilly and with sham protestations of benevolence. He sees him to be a canting hypocrite. He has previously come to the rake and spendthrift Charles, in the disguise of a broker, the friend of Moses the money-lender. What he sees and learns of Charles's character is told in the following scene; which, for liveliness, variety, wit, humour, knowledge of the world, as well as for a touch of deeper feeling than the older comedy knows, is quite unrivalled in English play writing.

CHARLES SURFACE'S House.

Enter TRIP, Sir OLIVER SURFACE, and MOSES.

Trip. Here, Master Moses! if you 'll stay a moment, I 'll try whether—what 's the gentleman's name?

Sir Ol. Aside. Mr. Moses, what is my name?

Moses. Mr. Premium.

Trip. Premium—very well.

Exit TRIP, *taking snuff.*

Sir Ol. To judge by the servants, one wouldn't believe the master was ruined. But what!—sure, this was my brother's house?

Moses. Yes, sir; Mr. Charles bought it of Mr. Joseph, with the furniture, pictures, etc., just as the old gentleman left it. Sir Peter thought it a piece of extravagance in him.

Sir Ol. In my mind, the other's economy in selling it to him was more reprehensible by half.

Enter TRIP.

Trip. My master says you must wait, gentlemen: he has company, and can't speak with you yet.

Sir Ol. If he knew who it was that wanted to see him, perhaps he would not send such a message?

Trip. Yes, yes, sir; he knows you are here—I did not forget little Premium: no, no, no.

Sir Ol. Very well; and I pray, sir, what may be your name?

Trip. Trip, sir; my name is Trip, at your service.

Sir Ol. Well then, Mr. Trip, you have a pleasant sort of place here, I guess?

Trip. Why, yes—here are three or four of us pass our time agreeably enough; but then our wages are sometimes a little in arrear—and not very great either—but fifty pounds a year, and find our own bags and bouquets.

Sir Ol. Aside. Bags and bouquets! Halters and bastinadoes!

Trip. And, à-propos, Moses—have you been able to get me that little bill discounted?

Sir Ol. Aside. Wants to raise money, too!—Mercy on me! Has his distresses too, I warrant, like a lord, and affects creditors and duns.

Moses. 'Twas not to be done, indeed, Mr. Trip.

Trip. Good lack, you surprise me! My friend Brush has indorsed it, and I thought when he put his name at the back of a bill 'twas the same as cash.

Moses. No! 'twouldn't do.

Trip. A small sum—but twenty pounds. Hark'ee, Moses—do you think you couldn't get it me by way of annuity?

Sir Ol. Aside. An annuity! Ha, ha! a footman raise money by way of annuity! Well done, luxury, egad!

Moses. Well, but you must ensure your place.

Trip. O, with all my heart! I'll ensure my place, and my life too, if you please.

Sir Ol. Aside. It's more than I would your neck.

Moses. But is there nothing you could deposit?

Trip. Why, nothing capital of my master's wardrobe has dropped lately; but I could give you a mortgage on some of his winter clothes, with equity of redemption before November—or you shall have the reversion of the French velvet, or a post-obit on the blue and silver;—these, I should think, Moses, with a few pair of point ruffles, as a collateral security—hey, my little fellow? *Bell rings.*

Moses. Well, well.

Trip. Egad, I heard the bell! I believe, gentlemen, I can now introduce you. Don't forget the annuity, little Moses! This way, gentlemen. I'll ensure my place, you know.

Sir Ol. If the man be a shadow of the master, this is the temple of dissipation indeed! *Exeunt.*

CHARLES SURFACE, CARELESS, Sir HARRY, *etc.,
at a table with wine, etc. Two Servants attending.*

Charles. 'Fore heaven, 'tis true! there's the great degeneracy of the age. Many of our acquaintance have taste, spirit, and politeness; but, plague on't, they won't drink.

Care. It is so indeed, Charles! They give-into all the substantial luxuries of the table, and abstain from nothing but wine and wit. O, certainly society suffers by it intolerably; for now, instead of the social spirit of raillery that used to mantle over a glass of bright Burgundy, their conversation is become just like the Spa water they drink, which has all the pertness and flatulence of Champagne, without the spirit or flavour.

Sir Toby. But what are they to do who love play better than wine?

Care. True: there's Sir Harry diets himself for gaming, and is now under a hazard regimen.

Charles. Then he'll have the worst of it. What! you wouldn't train a horse for the course by keeping him from corn? For my part, egad! I am never so successful as when I am a little merry. Let me throw on a bottle of Champagne, and I never lose—at least, I never feel my losses, which is exactly the same thing.

Sir Toby. Ay, that I believe.

Charles. And then, what man can pretend to be a believer in love, who is an adjurer of wine? 'Tis the test by which the lover knows his own heart. Fill a dozen bumpers to a dozen beauties, and she that floats atop is the maid that has bewitched you.

Care. Now then, Charles, be honest, and give us your real favourite.

Charles. Why, I have withheld her only in compassion to you. If I toast her, you must give a round of her peers, which is impossible—on earth.

Care. Oh, then we'll find some canonized vestals or heathen goddesses that will do, I warrant!

Charles. Here, then, bumpers, you rogues! bumpers! Maria! Maria!

Sir Harry. Maria who?

Charles. Oh, hang the surname—'tis too formal to

be registered in Love's calendar. Maria! But now, Sir Harry, beware, we must have beauty superlative.

Care. Nay, never study, Sir Harry; we'll stand to the toast, though your mistress should want an eye; and you know you have a song will excuse you.

Sir Harry. Egad, so I have! and I'll give him the song instead of the lady.

SONG.

Here's to the maiden of bashful fifteen;
   Here's to the widow of fifty;
Here's to the flaunting extravagant quean
   And here's to the housewife that's thrifty.
Chorus. *Let the toast pass,*
     Drink to the lass,
I warrant she'll prove an excuse for the glass.

Here's to the charmer whose dimples we prize,
   Now to the maid who has none, sir:
Here's to the girl with a pair of blue eyes,
   And here's to the nymph with but one, sir.
Chorus. *Let the toast pass, etc.*

Here's to the maid with a bosom of snow;
   Now to her that's as brown as a berry:
Here's to the wife with a face full of woe,
   And now to the girl that is merry.
Chorus. *Let the toast pass, etc.*

For let 'em be clumsy, or let 'em be slim,
Young or ancient, I care not a feather;
So fill a pint bumper quite up to the brim
And let us e'en toast them together.
Chorus. *Let the toast pass, etc.*

All. Bravo! bravo!

Enter TRIP, *and whispers* CHARLES SURFACE.

Charles. Gentlemen, you must excuse me a little. Careless, take the chair, will you?

Care. Nay, prithee, Charles, what now? This is one of your peerless beauties, I suppose, has dropt in by chance?

Charles. No, faith! To tell you the truth, 'tis a Jew and a broker, who are come by appointment.

Care. O! let's have the Jew in.

Sir Harry. Ay, and the broker too, by all means.

Care. Yes, yes, the Jew and the broker.

Charles. Egad, with all my heart! Trip, bid the gentlemen walk in—though there's one of them a stranger, I can tell you.

Care. Charles, let us give them some generous Burgundy, and perhaps they'll grow conscientious.

Charles. O, hang 'em, no! wine does but draw forth a man's natural qualities; and to make them drink would only be to whet their knavery.

Sir OLIVER SURFACE and MOSES.

Charles. So, honest Moses, walk in : walk in, pray, Mr. Premium—that's the gentleman's name, isn't it, Moses?

Moses. Yes, sir.

Charles. Set chairs, Trip—sit down, Mr. Premium—glasses, Trip—sit down, Moses. Come, Mr. Premium, I'll give you a sentiment; here's '*success to usury!*'—Moses, fill the gentleman a bumper.

Moses. Success to usury!

Care. Right, Moses—usury is prudence and industry, and deserves to succeed.

Sir Ol. Then—*here's all the success it deserves!*

Care. No, no, that won't do! Mr. Premium, you have demurred at the toast, and must drink it in a pint bumper.

Sir Harry. A pint bumper, at least.

Moses. O pray, sir, consider—Mr. Premium's a gentleman.

Care. And therefore loves good wine.

Sir Toby. Give Moses a quart glass—this is mutiny, and a high contempt for the chair.

Care. Here, now for't! I'll see justice done, to the last drop of my bottle.

Sir Ol. Nay, pray, gentlemen—I did not expect this usage.

Charles. No, hang it, you shan't! Mr. Premium's a stranger.

Sir Ol. Odd! I wish I was well out of their company.

Care. Plague on 'em then!—if they don't drink, we'll not sit down with them. Come, Harry, the dice are in the next room—Charles, you'll join us when you have finished your business with the gentlemen?

Charles. I will! I will!— *Exeunt.* Careless!

Care. Returning. Well?

Charles. Perhaps I may want you.

Care. O, you know I am always ready : word, note, or bond, 'tis all the same to me. *Exit.*

Moses. Sir, this is Mr. Premium, a gentleman of the strictest honour and secrecy: and always performs what he undertakes. Mr. Premium, this is—

Charles. Pshaw! have done. Sir, my friend Moses is a very honest fellow, but a little slow at expression: he'll be an hour giving us our titles. Mr. Premium, the plain state of the matter is this: I am an extravagant young fellow who wants to borrow money—you I take to be a prudent old fellow, who have got money to lend.—I am blockhead enough to give fifty per cent. sooner than not have it ; and you, I presume, are rogue enough to take a hundred if you can get it. Now, sir, you see we are acquainted at once, and may proceed to business without further ceremony.

Sir Ol. Exceeding frank, upon my word.—I see, sir, you are not a man of many compliments.

Charles. Oh no, sir! plain dealing in business I always think best.

Sir Ol. Sir, I like you the better for it—however, you are mistaken in one thing; I have no money to lend, but I believe I could procure some of a friend; but then he's an unconscionable dog, isn't he, Moses?

Moses. But you can't help that.

Sir Ol. And must sell stock to accommodate you—mustn't he, Moses?

Moses. Yes, indeed! You know I always speak the truth, and scorn to tell a lie!

Charles. Right. People that speak truth generally do: but these are trifles, Mr. Premium. What! I know money isn't to be bought without paying for 't.

Sir Ol. Well—but what security could you give? You have no land, I suppose?

Charles. Not a mole-hill, nor a twig, but what's in the bough-pots out of the window!

Sir Ol. Nor any stock, I presume?

Charles. Nothing but live stock—and that's only a few pointers and ponies. But pray, Mr. Premium, are you acquainted at all with any of my connexions?

Sir Ol. Why, to say truth, I am.

Charles. Then you must know that I have a dev'lish rich uncle in the East Indies, Sir Oliver Surface, from whom I have the greatest expectations?

Sir Ol. That you have a wealthy uncle I have heard; but how your expectations will turn out is more, I believe, than you can tell.

Charles. O no!—there can be no doubt. They tell me I'm a prodigious favourite, and that he talks of leaving me every thing.

Sir Ol. Indeed! this is the first I've heard of it.

Charles. Yes, yes, 'tis just so—Moses knows 'tis true—don't you, Moses?

Moses. O yes! I'll swear to 't.

Sir Ol. Aside. Egad, they'll persuade me presently I'm at Bengal.

Charles. Now I propose, Mr. Premium, if it's agreeable to you, a post-obit on Sir Oliver's life; though at the same time the old fellow has been so liberal to me, that I give you my word, I should be very sorry to hear that anything had happened to him.

Sir Ol. Not more than I should, I assure you. But the bond you mention happens to be just the worst security you could offer me—for I might live to a hundred, and never see the principal.

Charles. O yes, you would—the moment Sir Oliver dies, you know, you would come on me for the money.

Sir Ol. Then I believe I should be the most unwelcome dun you ever had in your life.

Charles. What! I suppose you're afraid that Sir Oliver is too good a life?

Sir Ol. No, indeed, I am not; though I have heard

T

he is as hale and healthy as any man of his years in christendom.

Charles. There again now you are misinformed. No, no, the climate has hurt him considerably, poor uncle Oliver! Yes, yes, he breaks apace, I'm told—and is so much altered lately, that his nearest relations don't know him.

Sir Ol. No! ha! ha! ha! so much altered lately, that his nearest relations don't know him! ha! ha! ha! egad—ha! ha! ha!

Charles. Ha! ha!—you're glad to hear that, little Premium?

Sir Ol. No, no, I'm not.

Charles. Yes, yes, you are—ha! ha! ha!—You know that mends your chance.

Sir Ol. But I'm told Sir Oliver is coming over?—nay, some say he is actually arrived?

Charles. Pshaw! Sure I must know better than you whether he's come or not. No, no, rely on't he's at this moment at Calcutta—isn't he, Moses.

Moses. O yes, certainly.

Sir Ol. Very true, as you say, you must know better than I, though I have it from pretty good authority—haven't I, Moses!

Moses. Yes, most undoubted!

Sir Ol. But, sir, as I understand you want a few hundreds immediately—is there nothing you could dispose of?

Charles. How do you mean?

Sir Ol. For instance, now, I have heard that your father left behind him a great quantity of massy old plate?

Charles. O Lud!—that's gone long ago.—Moses can tell you how, better than I can.

Sir Ol. Aside. Good lack! all the family race cups and corporation bowls!—*Aloud.* Then it was also supposed that his library was one of the most valuable and compact—

Charles. Yes, yes, so it was—vastly too much so for a private gentleman. For my part, I was always of a communicative disposition, so I thought it a shame to keep so much knowledge to myself.

Sir Ol. Mercy upon me! Learning that had run in the family like an heirloom! Pray, what are become of the books.

Charles. You must inquire of the auctioneer, Master Premium, for I don't believe even Moses can direct you.

Moses. I know nothing of books.

Sir Ol. So, so, nothing of the family property left, I suppose!

Charles. Not much, indeed; unless you have a mind to the family pictures. I have got a room full of ancestors above, and if you have a taste for paintings, egad, you shall have 'em a bargain.

Sir Ol. Hey! what the devil! sure, you wouldn't sell your forefathers, would you?

Charles. Every man of them to the best bidder.

Sir Ol. What! your great uncles and aunts?

Charles. Ay, and my great grandfathers and grandmothers too.

Sir Ol. Aside. Now I give him up. What the plague, have you no bowels for your own kindred? Odd's life, do you take me for Shylock in the play, that you would raise money of me on your own flesh and blood?

Charles. Nay, my little broker, don't be angry: what need you care if you have your money's worth?

Sir Ol. Well, I'll be the purchaser: I think I can dispose of the family canvas. *Aside.* Oh, I'll never forgive him this! never!

Enter CARELESS.

Care. Come, Charles, what keeps you?

Charles. I can't come yet: i' faith we are going to have a sale above stairs; here's little Premium will buy all my ancestors.

Care. O, burn your ancestors!

Charles. No, he may do that afterwards, if he pleases. Stay, Careless, we want you: egad, you shall be auctioneer; so come along with us.

Care. O, have with you, if that's the case. Handle a hammer as well as a dice-box!

Sir Ol. Aside. Oh, the profligates!

Charles. Come, Moses, you shall be appraiser, if we

want one. Gad's life, little Premium, you don't seem to like the business?

Sir Ol. O yes, I do, vastly. Ha, ha, ha ! yes, yes, I think it a rare joke to sell one's family by auction— ha, ha, ha ! *Aside.* O, the prodigal !

Charles. To be sure ! when a man wants money, where the plague should he get assistance if he can't make free with his own relations? *Exeunt.*

Picture Room at CHARLES'S.

Enter CHARLES SURFACE, *Sir* OLIVER SURFACE, MOSES, *and* CARELESS.

Charles. Walk in, gentlemen, pray walk in ;—here they are, the family of the Surfaces, up to the Conquest.

Sir Ol. And, in my opinion, a goodly collection.

Charles. Ay, ay, these are done in the true spirit of portrait painting ;—no *volontier grace* and expression. Not like the works of your modern Raphaels, who give you the strongest resemblance, yet contrive to make your portrait independent of you; so that you may sink the original and not hurt the picture.— No, no ; the merit of these is the inveterate likeness— all stiff and awkward as the originals, and like nothing in human nature besides.

Sir Ol. Ah ! we shall never see such figures of men again.

Charles. I hope not.—Well, you see, Master Premium, what a domestic character I am; here I sit of an evening surrounded by my family.—But, come, get to your pulpit, Mr. Auctioneer; here's an old gouty chair of my grandfather's will answer the purpose.

Care. Ay, ay, this will do.—But, Charles, I haven't a hammer; and what's an auctioneer without his hammer?

Charles. Egad, that's true;—what parchment have we here? O, our genealogy in full. Here, Careless,—you shall have no common bit of mahogany, here's the family tree for you, you rogue—this shall be your hammer, and now you may knock down my ancestors with their own pedigree.

Sir Ol. Aside. What an unnatural rogue!—an *ex post facto* parricide!

Care. Yes, yes, here's a bit of your generation indeed;—faith, Charles, this is the most convenient thing you could have found for the business, for 'twill serve not only as a hammer, but a catalogue into the bargain.—Come begin—A-going, a-going, a-going!

Charles. Bravo, Careless! Well, here's my great uncle, Sir Richard Raveline, a marvellous good general in his day, I assure you. He served in all the Duke of Marlborough's wars, and got that cut over his eye at the battle of Malplaquet.—What say you, Mr. Premium?—look at him—there's a hero, not cut out of his feathers, as your modern clipt captains are, but enveloped in wig and regimentals, as a general should be.—What do you bid?

Moses. Mr. Premium would have *you* speak.

Charles. Why, then, he shall have him for ten pounds, and I'm sure that's not dear for a staff-officer.

Sir Ol. Aside. Heaven deliver me! his famous uncle Richard for ten pounds!—Well, sir, I take him at that.

Charles. Careless, knock down my uncle Richard.— Here, now, is a maiden sister of his, my great aunt Deborah, done by Kneller, thought to be in his best manner, and a very formidable likeness.—There she is, you see—shepherdess feeding her flock.—You shall have her for five pounds ten—the sheep are worth the money.

Sir Ol. Aside. Ah! poor Deborah! a woman who set such a value on herself! Five pounds ten—she's mine.

Charles. Knock down my aunt Deborah!—Here, now, are two that were a sort of cousins of theirs. You see, Moses, these pictures were done some time ago, when beaux wore wigs, and the ladies their own hair.

Sir Ol. Yes, truly, head-dresses appear to have been a little lower in those days.

Charles. Well, take that couple for the same.

Moses. 'Tis good bargain.

Charles. Careless!—This, now, is a grandfather of

my mother's, a learned judge, well known on the western circuit. What do you rate him at, Moses?

Moses. Four guineas.

Charles. Four guineas! Gad's life, you don't bid me the price of his wig. Mr. Premium, you have more respect for the woolsack; do let us knock his lordship down at fifteen.

Sir Ol. By all means.

Care. Gone!

Charles. And there are two brothers of his, William and Walter Blunt, Esquires, both members of Parliament, and noted speakers; and what's very extraordinary, I believe this is the first time they were ever bought or sold.

Sir Ol. That is very extraordinary, indeed! I'll take them at your own price, for the honour of Parliament.

Care. Well said, little Premium! I'll knock them down at forty.

Charles. Here's a jolly fellow—I don't know what relation, but he was Mayor of Manchester. Take him at eight pounds.

Sir Ol. No, no; six will do for the mayor.

Charles. Come, make it guineas, and I'll throw you the two aldermen there into the bargain.

Sir Ol. They're mine.

Charles. Careless, knock down the mayor and aldermen.—But plague on 't, we shall be all day retailing in this manner ;—do let us deal wholesale : what say you, little Premium? Give me three hundred pounds for the rest of the family in the lump.

Care. Ay, ay, that will be the best way.

Sir Ol. Well, well, anything to accommodate you;— they are mine. But there is one portrait which you have always passed over.

Care. What, that ill-looking little fellow over the settee?

Sir Ol. Yes, sir, I mean that, though I don't think him so ill-looking a little fellow, by any means.

Charles. What, that?—Oh! that's my uncle Oliver; 'twas done before he went to India.

Care. Your uncle Oliver!—Gad, then you'll never be friends, Charles. That, now, to me, is as stern a looking rogue as ever I saw; an unforgiving eye, and a damned disinheriting countenance! An inveterate knave, depend on't. Don't you think so, little Premium?

Sir Ol. Upon my soul, sir, I do not: I think it is as honest a looking face as any in the room, dead or alive;—but I suppose uncle Oliver goes with the rest of the lumber?

Charles. No, hang it; I'll not part with poor Noll. The old fellow has been very good to me, and egad! I'll keep his picture while I've a room to put it in.

Sir Ol. Aside. The rogue's my nephew after all!—

But, sir, I have somehow taken a fancy to that picture.

Charles. I'm sorry for 't, for you certainly will not have it.—Oons, haven't you got enough of them?

Sir Ol. Aside. I forgive him everything!—But, sir, when I take a whim in my head I don't value money. I'll give you as much for that as for all the rest.

Charles. Don't tease me, master broker; I tell you I'll not part with it, and there's an end of it.

Sir Ol. Aside. How like his father the dog is!—Well, well, I have done. *Aside.*—I did not perceive it before, but I think I never saw such a striking resemblance.—Here is a draught for your sum.

Charles. Why, 'tis for eight hundred pounds.

Sir Ol. You will not let Sir Oliver go?

Charles. Zounds! no!—I tell you once more.

Sir Ol. Then never mind the difference—we'll balance that another time—but give me your hand on the bargain; you are an honest fellow, Charles—I beg pardon, sir, for being so free.—Come, Moses.

Charles. Egad, this is a whimsical old fellow! But hark'ee, Premium—you'll prepare lodgings for these gentlemen?

Sir Ol. Yes, yes; I'll send for them in a day or two.

Charles. But hold; do now send a genteel conveyance for them, for I assure you they were most of them used to ride in their own carriages.

Sir Ol. I will, I will—for all but Oliver?

Charles. Ay, all but the little nabob.

Sir Ol. You 're fixed on that?

Charles. Peremptorily.

Sir Ol. Aside. A dear extravagant rogue!—Good day!—Come, Moses.—Let me hear now who calls him profligate!

www.ingramcontent.com/pod-product-compliance
Lightning Source LLC
Chambersburg PA
CBHW022027240426
43667CB00042B/1217